D1474131

GOD LOVES ME AND I LOVE MYSELF!

Overcoming the Resistance to Loving Yourself

Mark DeJesus

Please note the writing style in this book chooses to capitalize certain pronouns in Scripture that refer to God the Father, the Son, and the Holy Spirit, and may differ from other publishing styles. Web Sites that are referenced were up to date at the time of publishing and are not endorsed unless specifically stated so in the writing.

God Loves Me and I Love Myself!
Overcoming the Resistance to Loving Yourself
By Mark DeJesus
Turning Hearts Ministries & Transformed You
www.markdejesus.com
Copyright 2016 – Mark DeJesus & Turning Hearts Ministries

Published by: Turning Hearts Ministries

ISBN-13: 978-1539307501

ISBN-10:1539307506

Cover Design: Ryan Louse and 99designs.com

Editorial Assistance Provided by:
Rick McKinniss, Eileen Gonzalez, Chris Fields, Stan Doll, Melissa DeJesus

CONTENTS

Dedication

I dedicate this book to my children, Maximus and Abigail, who will grow up learning to love themselves as God loves them; taking the Father's heart to every area of influence He calls them to. You both are overcomers.

Acknowledgements

I want to acknowledge and thank my wife Melissa, who has processed countless challenges with me and has walked with me every step as we developed our journey of loving ourselves. God placed the perfect woman in my life to take this journey with.

I also want to thank Chris Fields, who took my first manuscript draft and challenged me to take it to the next level. Her input imparted to me the precise steps needed to take this message to the next level. I am so grateful to you for that.

Introduction

Imagine you are living during the times of Christ here on earth. You have discovered this great Man of God who is healing the sick, cleansing the lepers and even raising the dead. Nothing seems to faze Him and everything He touches, changes. He has answers that speak to the heart of mankind's deepest needs and does it with a love not seen in history.

The scenes that unfold before you are fascinating, therefore you cannot stop watching. Masses are being dramatically touched left and right. There is something about Him that makes you want to be near Him.

As soon as you hear where He's going to be, you feverishly push through the crowd, doing all you can to get as close as possible. Scanning the horizon through the crowds of people, you spot a glimpse of Him, standing by a hillside, using the valley as a way to let His voice travel. You inch closer so that you don't have to strain your hearing to catch His words. Everything He speaks has such profound weight, you are processing His words as fast as your heart can take it in.

As He teaches, Jesus addresses a question coming from the religious people in the audience. Someone asks, *what is the greatest commandment? What's most important in the law?* In other words, they're asking, *we cannot remember every beautiful nugget You have shared, so what is the key takeaway we need to know?* They were looking for a simple, bottom-line answer.

In response, Jesus shares the treasure of the Kingdom in just a few short sentences; illuminating to people what life with God is all about. His answer completely revolved around love and relationships.

Jesus said to him, "You shall love the Lord your God with all your heart, with all your soul, and with all your mind." This is the first and great commandment. And the second is like it: "You shall love your neighbor as yourself." On these two commandments hang all the Law and the Prophets.
Matthew 22:37-40

To sum up the answer to their questions in one phrase, it would be *love* . . . love God, love yourself, love people. Pretty straight forward, right?

There is just one problem. If I were there, I would need some help understanding the application of this precept. Amidst the throngs of people, I would immediately raise my hand. Slightly nervous, yet hungry to learn, I wouldn't let my trembling hands impede my hunger for learning. In the politest manner possible, I would interject a question with the hope that more explanation could be given.

Great Teacher! I am stuck on something, if you don't mind.

The statement, AS yourself. . .

You mentioned we are to love our neighbor AS ourselves.

Can you elaborate on that?

How do we even do that?

Are you with me on this? How does one know how to love one's self? If anyone is honest, most would admit to not knowing what it even means to love yourself.

What does loving yourself look like? I would ask Jesus, "Could you talk a little more about what that entails? Basically what I am getting here is that I am to love my neighbor in direct proportion to how I am able to love myself? I don't know how to do that! I don't even know where to start. Plus, I am a guy. How does a guy know how to love himself?"

How would you answer this question?

NO REFERENCES

Growing up I had no comprehension for what healthy self-love was. In fact, nowhere did I even find a value for it. Most of what I heard was preaching and teaching that gave us a good beating; where self-rejecting messages were considered spiritual. Words of "crucify" and "deny" were used in a way to beat us down in any way possible. "Dying to self" subtly became hating of self. Christian living became a monastery of believers living in a war against themselves all day long.

Even the thought of self-love was never embraced. Most testimonies were laden with words of contempt and loathing of one's self; giving little room for self-acceptance or value. Fasting, praying and Bible reading were all seen as opportunities to thoroughly beat ourselves up. It was even seen as admirable. The more we did it, the more spiritual we were. All of this was done in the name of a, "He must increase, I must decrease" religious exercise. It is as if being negative about ourselves was viewed with high esteem.

I followed some very well-known preachers that would promote this kind of living. Their well-intentioned messages had amazing truth about the cross, sacrifice and dying to self. I gained so much. But hidden within the fabric of those homilies were threads of self-hatred, self-rejection and self-accusation. Yet so many never noticed it, because the leaders looked so spiritual to the undiscerning view.

To these orators, self-love was seen as arrogant. A heavy fear weighed on Christians, worried that if someone "loved" himself or herself, they would fall into pride. Fearing the work of arrogance in our lives, many dove into a pool of self-beating mindsets. We feared being prideful so much we actually ended up in pride. We rejected the importance of loving and accepting ourselves as God's creation.

If God tells us to love our neighbor as we love ourselves, wouldn't it be disobedient and prideful to NOT love yourself? Self-love does not seem like a suggestion, but a command. Has our inability to love ourselves properly even twisted what pride and arrogance look like? It seems the greatest commandment is actually the most un-followed?

I remember as a young man, hearing a pastor say, "We all know how to love ourselves, because we are all so selfish!" Self-love to him was arrogant and selfish. Yet true biblical love is not self-absorbed. In fact, when the Bible warns about people being "lovers of themselves" it describes those that became self-absorbed.

The very nature of love looks outward, from a place where one has received love. We give out from what we possess. If we love ourselves properly, we give out what we have freely received. If we are loved but don't give it out, love has been misunderstood. When we struggle relationally, it often goes back to how well we are able to receive God's love and process that for ourselves.

Unfortunately, many are loving people out of how they love themselves . . . *terribly*! Yet this issue will not be resolved by attempting to love others better. We can only give out of what we have received. The emphasis needs to shift, where people place more value on learning to receive love so they can give out of that precious gift to all mankind in greater power.

A MODERN PLAGUE

The majority of our relationship issues stem from our struggles to love and accept ourselves. Relationships make the world go round. Everything rises and falls on the quality of our relationships. We cannot make improvements, while ignoring the real problem. Because we have not taken the love of God for ourselves, and it is affecting everything.

Try walking by a full-length mirror. Take a look at yourself without any negativity. Gaze into your reflection without picking apart something about yourself. It's pretty hard to do, right? Very few people walk by a mirror, and are ok with what they see. Even the most beautiful people on the cover of magazines struggle with their reflection.

Well Mark that's just normal. Everyone does that!

Everyone may have battles with it, but do we all need to remain stuck in this problem? Is that what God really created us with? An unending flurry of thoughts that negatively beat up who we are, how we look and what we sound like? There must be a better way.

We get hung up on our appearance. Our voice sounds stupid to us. We're too fat, too tall, old looking, flabby. These thoughts never end. We have been veiled over with a hate-filled set of eyeglasses as we see ourselves. Our eyes have been trained to accuse rather than affirm.

Most people have been trained to be hard on themselves, to live as their own worst enemy, and remain in a daily heavyweight match against themselves. Their self-talk and inner dialogue never let them enter into peace and rest. This all stems from an inability to love ourselves. Love is the answer, but we keep dodging it like there must be something else missing.

Husbands don't know how to love their wives. Wives struggle to love their husbands. A lack of self-love is deeply affecting our marriages. Friends struggle to have healthy connection, because their self-love issues interfere with the free flow of love in the relationship. Instead of serving each other freely, everyone looks out for themselves in survival and self-protection.

MY NEED FOR FREEDOM

Of all the subjects I have taught on, this one hits home the most. My entire life was filled with an inability to love and accept myself. I am not writing this book from theory, but from a place of personal experience. My own healing and the lives of those I have been able to touch have created a template for everything that is written in this book.

For too long, I lived with an inability to love myself. Yet it took a very long time for me to see the problem. My relational insecurities and fears put me into a spiritual and emotional prison where I could not connect intimately and freely with others. I desperately longed to connect, but didn't know how to feel safe in that dynamic.

I carried a resistance towards loving myself, but couldn't identify the problem. Unknowingly, I covered over my lack of self-love with a lifestyle neck deep in performance and attempts to earn love. My empty heart sought for approval and acceptance in what I did, but was never fulfilled. No manner of achieving ever fulfilled the relational love I craved. Perfectionism, people pleasing and endless drivenness all led me back to the dark void in my life.

The inability to love myself showed up in my relationships. I was in a continual state of never being able to settle into safe connection. It was like I had a Plexiglas wall on my chest, keeping me from landing safely into love. When I met Melissa and wanted to draw close, my bondage rose up to a heightened level, once again. It was at this point I arrived at a critical crossroads of life. I had to make a decision. *Was I going to live alone in a prison of isolation and insanity or was I willing to take personal responsibility to get free?*

I'm glad I made the right decision, because it led me into a journey of freedom from the chains that kept me from loving myself and, loving others freely. But it took an all-out investment to do so. No more playing games. No more living as a child. I had to become a man and face the war in my heart.

MY GIFT TO YOU

In my journey of becoming free, I made a promise to God:

"If you will set me free, I will take everything You teach me and share with everyone who will listen."

Therefore, this book is written to set your heart free in love and to come into peace with yourself. My prayer is that you will see that you need to love yourself like your life, health and destiny all depend on it. Because it does!

01

What is Self-Love?

You shall love your neighbor as yourself.
- Jesus, Matthew 22:39

He who loves his wife loves himself.
Ephesians 5:28

One Saturday afternoon, a group of eager attendees, including myself, gathered at a seminar to experience healing and wholeness in a deeper way. Our hearts were hungry and I was desperate to break through some hindrances I battled. Although emotionally open, I had little idea as to what I would encounter that day. Searching for answers, yet clueless in how to find them, my brokenness was about to make a divine collision with love.

Each session built on the previous. We were all drawn into allowing God to heal the broken areas of our lives. At the closing of one particular session, a female leader stood to the front to offer words of healing for all those present. In that moment, we could feel the atmosphere shift. Our hearts were open to receive and we knew we were about to experience something powerful.

Her eyes were calm and gentle; her voice soft and quietening.

Old enough to be my grandmother, I was quickly able to lean into the emotional safety she established in the room. There was a tender and nurturing presence she carried in her voice. Each word was saturated with healing, reconciliation and approval. It was evident to all who were present; this was from the very heart of God.

She was thoughtful in her approach to make eye contact with each person present. As her eyes moved in my direction, she proceeded to look right at me and speak into my pain. She knew nothing of my journey, nor of the brokenness I struggled with. Yet, it didn't matter. God was using her to speak into my heart.

Without any chance to hyper analyze, my heart was immediately touched in a way I never expected. God used this woman's words to infiltrate a deep wound in my heart that had never been reached. As I dropped to my knees and tears poured out, I knew I had just collided with a fresh experience of healing love.

I had brokenness in my heart that did not allow me to love myself. Friends and loved ones knew I carried this wound. I knew I was broken, but like many others, I searched all over, thinking the issue had not yet been discovered. But it was right in front of me. Her words that day brought out the pain and initiated a chain reaction of healing in the years following.

Sometimes our biggest struggles seem hidden, but are right in front of us in plain view. Masses of people are being blocked from the beauty of loving themselves and don't even know it. Sadly, most do not even see the need to talk about it.

It's not until much heartache has been experienced and personal crisis has exploded that people even entertain the subject of whether or not they love themselves. Most do not even *like* themselves, but they've been conditioned to cover that up.

My biggest challenge in working with people is helping them see the problem that is driving the spider web of issues in their lives. Deep down, the battle has to do with how they process love for themselves. It manifests in every area of their life, affecting how they do life and relationships, but they often don't see the connection.

Most attempt to manage with social cover-ups & fabrications while others openly sink in its grip. Regardless of how people attempt to cope, masses are wandering through life with bondage that is hurting themselves. This war keeps them blocked from seeing themselves the way God sees them and loving themselves the way God loves them. Freedom is available, but they often don't even realize it.

It can be easy to avoid pain and the emptiness in our hearts. The enormity of how much we lack self-love can go unnoticed for quite some time. We will continue to live ignorantly until our pain screams so loud that we are then forced to face ourselves and the void in our hearts.

In my calling of helping people overcome, I have found a lack of self-love tops the charts on the list of battlegrounds they face. I believe we cannot avoid it much longer. God is leading us to face this issue in a heart to heart manner so that our land can experience the needed healing.

Here's the problem. I am pinpointing a subject most people do not even have a reference for. I am addressing a need most people didn't even know they carried. We all want to be loved, but we were never taught the importance of loving ourselves the way God loves us. That's why I believe this book could save your life.

WHAT I AM NOT SAYING

Before you come up with your own conclusions, allow me to explain what true self-love is in its purest form, by first explaining what self-love is *not*. I would hate to begin on a faulty definition or perspective. Because this topic is alien to most, allow me to bring clarification by showing you what self-love is not.

1. Self-centered. Focusing solely on one's self with little regard for others, has nothing to do with self-love and is more self-idolatry. Selfishness and self-centeredness are counterfeits that are not concerned with loving others authentically, but elevating one's self. True love says, I am willing to lay down my life for another.

Those who are narcissistic are not operating from the heart of true self-love. They live what is often referred to as an ego-centric reality, where life to them is all about themselves. Narcissists find ways to remain in a selfish world that is vain, spending very little time thinking or empathizing over others. Many who say they love themselves are often typical narcissists because they make most situations, conversations and scenarios circle back to themselves. Their emphasis always seems to be what's going on with them, their viewpoint and their feelings.

People who love themselves properly give it out right away. They spend little time obsessing over their own life. Once love is received, it naturally goes out. They have settled love in their hearts, so it flows out very freely.

2. Self-indulgent. Many times I hear from well-intentioned people who share examples of how they are "loving themselves." Yet they deliver tales of foolish financial decisions and endless hours of wasteful activities, all with a label of self-love. This is not what I am speaking of. Eating a tub of ice cream and checking out with television is not self-love. It's actually a manifestation of lacking self-love, because those experiences do not add life. In fact, those habits can often drive people further into unhealthy emotional prisons.

3. Self-exaltation. Years ago, I remember watching someone who was working overtime to draw attention to himself. He went out of his way to make sure people were noticing him. I overheard an observer say, "Well that guy really loves himself." This is a classic mistake. He doesn't. He actually hates himself, but needs extra attention to fill a void in his heart. He exerts extra energy to feel the affirmation of people's eyes observing him. This is not self-love.

4. Self-pity. Scores of people live as victims, where their life has been defined by their limitations. This victim mindset has become a modern plague over our generation. Victims become bombarded with problems so much, they find themselves imprisoned by them. Without healthy self-love, they confuse self-pity as a way to comfort themselves. Convinced that no one is showing them love, they seek to comfort themselves by bringing attention to their pain. They see it as comforting themselves, yet it becomes a personal immersion into their problems and woes.

Instead of loving on those around, they become isolated in

their own trouble, leaving them emotionally unavailable to others. They may think they are "loving themselves" when in reality they are trapped in a prison as victims. This mindset is light-years away from self-love. In fact, self-pity is an absolute counterfeit.

DISCOVERING SELF-LOVE

When we truly receive God's love in our hearts, we step into the arena where loving ourselves is possible. The Bible reminds us that *we love Him because He first loved us[1]*. Father God is the initiator of love. He broadcasts who He is as love to us, with an invitation to love Him back. The fruitfulness of our love relationship with God relies on our hearts receiving the love that is transmitted from heaven.

It is imperative to know that loving ourselves is predicated on receiving the unending love that God has for us. We cannot love God until we have first received it from Him and allowed that love to permeate how we see ourselves. The love that God pours out empowers us to see ourselves through that love. Therefore, we can know we have plugged into God's love when we are able to love ourselves properly.

But what does it actually mean to live in healthy self-love?

Loving yourself allows you to see yourself the way God sees you. In thoughts, words and actions, you are able to relate to yourself from a motivation of love. Self-love involves a healthy acceptance of yourself, right where you are, with no strings

---

[1] 1 John 4:19

attached. You are at peace to be yourself, because this is the environment that self-love creates. Your pattern of living flows from a pure reflection of God's love for you.

Self-love defines how you find acceptance in life, communicating you are accepted right where you are. It keeps you rooted in a sense of belonging that is not based on merit or performance. Whether you are surrounded by a crowd of affirming people or sitting quietly in solitude, self-love keeps you satisfied in the arms of God's acceptance.

Self-love sets the tone for how you establish your worth in life. When you love yourself properly, you gain a healthy sense of value, based on the simplicity of being loved. It grounds your worth in the sacrifice of Jesus Christ, who gave of His life for you as a love gift. His death and resurrection gave you the opportunity to become Father God's treasured child. Therefore, it has nothing to do with your roles or achievement, but in simply accepting the invitation to be God's kid. Performance cannot enhance the love a Father has for His child. So growing in self-love is founded upon the ability of a child learning to receive love.

Self-love manifests best when you engage the pillars of love, patience and kindness, towards yourself. Love is patient and is kind[1]. Being immersed in self-love involves being patient and kind in all your thoughts and actions towards yourself.

With self-love, you are able to engage in the power of love, whether other people love you or not. Your self-esteem and identity are not hinged on every act of others. If they happen to extend love to you in an authentic way, it is a bonus to the love

---

[1] 1 Corinthians 13:4

you already possess from God. This does not imply that self-love ignores relationship. In fact, it enhances connection, because it releases you from many relationship hang-ups that are based on self-love's absence.

Self-love cultivates a healthy acceptance of your flaws and imperfections. It does not obsess over those areas that many people hide every day. Loving yourself affirms the invitation for authenticity, where you can be yourself, eliminating the fear of exposure and condemnation. Healthy self-love allows you to live accepted, safe and at peace in your own skin.

When you operate in healthy self-love, affirming what God says about you becomes a byproduct. Self-love says, "I choose to love what God loves. He loves me! So therefore, I love myself."

Loving yourself has a lot to do with self-compassion, giving to yourself what you would often extend to someone whom you love dearly. Many people live kindly towards others, but never give that level of kindness to themselves. They may exercise patience with others, but rarely live in that dimension of patience when they look in the mirror. No wonder they eventually burn out. They've been living and giving from an empty tank. Loving yourself satisfies the deep longing of your heart while establishing a powerful reservoir of compassion to pour out to others.

A RELATIONSHIP WITH YOURSELF

In order to manifest the fruit of self-love, you have to cultivate a healthy relationship with yourself. Many do not even see this as something worth investing in. They ignore tending to their own needs or spend endless years being negative and hard on themselves. Others live in wild insecurity and many become numb to the pain of their heart. This leads many to a burned out, depressed and empty life. Self-love says, "You were made for more than that."

I love restoring people into a healthy relationship with themselves, but many have never even considered it. You spend more time with you than anyone else on the planet. Wouldn't it be a good idea for you to learn to walk in love towards yourself, so you can make the most of your life?

Whether you like it or not, you do have a relationship with yourself. In fact, you are with yourself all day long. Although millions attempt to, you cannot escape yourself. No geographic change or drug escape can release you from the fact that you still have to deal with yourself. Why not invest in learning to love yourself and engage healthier patterns in how you face being you?

THE FLOW OF LOVE

There are three relationships we cultivate every day that need to be nurtured in love. These three are a relationship with (1) God, (2) ourselves and (3) others.

First, God's love flows to us so that we can receive what we were eternally designed to carry—the glorious love and acceptance of our heavenly Father. Because of the work of Christ, we can see the divine demonstration of God's love.

It is then our response to receive His love; to say *yes* to His life changing and never-ending love. If we truly receive Father

God's love, then we are able to love Him back effectively and freely. Any attempt to love God without first receiving His love is unfruitful. We can only love God out of the love we have received from Him. God *is* love, so if we need love, we need to encounter Him. He is very the source and essence of love to fill our lives. We cannot even begin to love Him without first receiving love from Him as our Father. Otherwise loving God becomes entirely based on religious striving.

Many seek to love God through performance but God's love cannot be earned. Unfortunately, many see a love relationship with God as doing "stuff" for Him. When we feel distant from God, our default response is often to do more, serve more and engage more religious duty.

This all changed for me once I learned to stop and first seek to receive God's love. His unconditional love for me is not based on anything I have done or will ever do. His love for me is present because I am His child. A loving parent doesn't have to explain why they love their children--they just do. It is the same with our Father in heaven.

Without receiving the Father's love for us, we will waste a lifetime trying to love God from an empty tank. This is where we must change our focus. We need to move to positioning ourselves for being filled up with God's love. Then out of what we have received, we love Him back with deep gratitude and passion.

It is out of this love we have received, that we then love on others. Love is not meant to sit stagnant. It must flow out. When we truly love ourselves the way God designed us to, that love will immediately flow out to bless mankind. Attempts to love others without receiving God's love for one's self eventually leads to severe burnout. We must first learn to love ourselves in order to effectively love others in the long run.

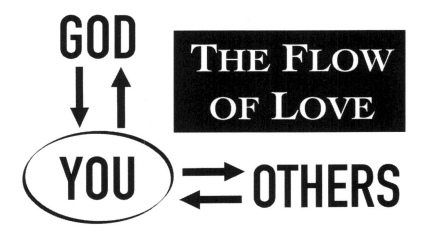

UNCLOGGING THE FLOW OF LOVE

The Bible beautifully reveals narratives, precepts and revelations that depict how to do relationship on all 3 levels; with God, with you and with others. For the flow to go well, we must learn to have a great relationship with ourselves. We do this by receiving God's love, but it also includes receiving love from other people. We often emphasize a love relationship with God, but push aside the importance of love relationships with others.

It isn't until we confront the brokenness in our hearts that change will occur in all three relationships. When the heart is impacted, we discover the keys to being more fully engaged in love. In the next chapter, I want to go deeper and empower the heart to experience love, so we can see life change occur in the fullest way possible.

QUESTIONS FOR CONSIDERATION

1. Do you have a great relationship with yourself? Where do you feel God is seeking to deepen your understanding of His love for you?

2. In what ways do you see that self-love has been absent from your life?

3. Growing up, how did a lack of self-love affect your own upbringing?

4. In the flow of love, where are you experiencing the biggest block?

PRAYER
Read This Prayer Out Loud

Father God, I want to live a healthier life of love. I open my heart today to experience more of that love. I recognize there is a deeper dimension of Your love that needs to invade my heart. So I position myself to receive from You. I am becoming more aware of how I try to love You without first receiving Your love. Help me to position myself to saying "yes" to Your love and let it flow into the very fiber of my being. I want to learn to receive from You. Let Your perfect love work in my life, in the ways You know I need the most. I open my heart to You God and to all the love that You are. In Jesus name, amen.

02

The Heart of the Matter

Keep your heart with all diligence, for out of it spring the
issues of life.
Proverbs 4:23

I stood there as a high level ministry leader began to break down right in front of me. He had hit a level of burnout, where his way of living was catching up to him. He began to weep, as if an emotional switch had instantly been triggered. Through the tears, he expressed the dryness and unfulfilled state he lived in. Everything he shared confirmed that he had neglected the life of his heart. He was giving of himself fully to the work he was involved in, but had lost his compass in receiving love for himself and nurturing his identity.

He had been locked in the daily grind, constant busyness and endless demands, which prohibited him from connecting to the self-love his heart needed. It is astounding how we are able to produce so much in activity but very little in the quality of our hearts.

Yet something remarkable happened after he poured out those tears in front me. As quickly as he looked like he was having a nervous breakdown, that switch of tears was immediately turned off. Something took over to put him back into his previous mode. He dried his eyes, looked up and said, "I'm fine. I'm going to be ok." Just like that he walked away and went back to the same life.

He was deceived. He was not fine and things were not ok. He had no compass to deal with the pain of his heart. So he did what most do, he shoved it down. He exemplified what many leaders, businessmen, parents, husbands and wives all seem to do today, ignore the issues of the heart, because the show must go on. Meanwhile, so many are eroding inside because they have neglected the life of the heart and the importance of self-love.

I wish there was a happy ending to that story, but this man's life went into some dead end traps that stole the life of his heart and robbed his potential. Unfortunately, I have watched this pattern occur over and over. When the heart does not experience self-love a regular basis, our lives suffer and those around us miss out on our full potential.

INVESTING IN THE LIFE OF YOUR HEART

The big question here is; *do you really want to work on loving yourself?* I am not asking if you can act loving towards others. Can you truly process love in your heart for yourself? Do you know how to receive love from God so that the needs of your heart are satisfied every day?

If we desire change in this area, we must first see loving ourselves as a foundational priority. Otherwise we will continue to fall back on old references that keep us from experiencing love and life. Without an "all-in" personal investment, the heart will never be *in-it-to-win-it*. It is the heart that becomes impacted by our priorities. The treasures we live for manifest in what our life displays.

What began my personal transformation was an awakening to my heart's need to be healed. My desire was to experience love in a deeper way. It first took a humbling of my heart and an openness to engaging love in a way I never had. I began the process of slowing down and facing my life. I had to stop jumping to all my faulty and sometimes goofy coping mechanisms. I believe you will need to do the same to experience genuine freedom.

Sit down with someone and ask them, "How's your heart?" Most people struggle to answer, because they spend little time thinking about the condition of their heart. Many are uncomfortable even talking about heart issues, because they spend their day in surface level interactions.

We cannot ignore our heart issues forever, because eventually they will chase us down. We can get away with skipping over them for a while, but eventually the unaddressed issues will rise up and take us on for size. It may be a crisis, an emotional collapse or a breakdown in the body where illness manifests. Either way, it's better that we face what we need to now. If we are willing to press in, despite the discomfort, I promise, change is on the way.

THE HEART NOT THE HEAD

The heart needs to experience love transformation, not just the mind. Today, most principles are taught in classrooms, where information exchange is often the priority. Speeches fill our lives. In fact, when parents correct their children, it is often through a lecture. This has left our hearts neglected, because the heart is changed through experience, not just knowledge alone.

Love cannot be understood through learning information alone. The nature of it is far deeper than that. Ask a parent why they love their child. Ask a bride why she loves her husband to be. The answers will vary, but what you hear will be expressions from the heart. We can attempt to explain love, but eventually we have to experience it.

The key to self-love is recognizing that our heart needs an *experience* of love. I believe not just once, but over and over. This is not just a head or mind issue. Jesus did not come to heal the broken-headed, but the broken hearted. When it comes to the heart, we cannot just think our way into a love encounter. We must position our hearts to be loved.

In today's self-help culture, we want to read "five quick tips" or "three hacks to change your life" and "seven steps to change." But that does not position the heart for change. It only gives us more information. Knowledge alone does not lead to transformation unless the heart experiences what knowledge points to.

The Bible has much to say about the heart, for out of it flow all the issues of life[1]. If the spiritual heart is healthy, it will have a compounding effect of health in our whole being. The heart was designed to be filled with love--love from God, love for God, love for self and for others.

---

[1] Proverbs 4:23

Modern culture makes its biggest investment to the mind, because it's easier to learn information than it is to deal with heart issues. When addressing the heart, you have to face both sadness and joy; sorrow and rejoicing; love and rejection; pain and pleasure. When we invest in our hearts, we become willing to patiently walk through what love means and process it. Most people are not comfortable with that. Therefore, their hearts are left unattended.

In the Old Testament, there was no word used for *the mind*. Instead, the word *heart* was utilized in the Hebrew language. Later on, the Greeks brought and emphasized the word *mind*, leading to mankind's elevation of head knowledge over heart cultivation. The word *mind* can at times can take the focus off of the heart, causing us to mentally figure everything out rather than experiencing truth deeply.

In the Old Testament culture, the emphasis of learning was based on participation with what was learned, not just sitting in lectures and ingesting bits of information. When we learn from the heart, we make contact with knowledge and process truth through our life as our way of learning. Powerful belief is formed and faith is ignited greatly.

In order to gain something in our heart, we have to practice something to really possess it. One does not "know" something until knowledge has been experienced in real life. Very few know how to cultivate heart learning. We are so used to just hearing lectures and speeches with little life application.

Tending to the life of the heart takes time and experience. This is a major reason why society is getting "brain smarter" and "heart dumber" over the years. We have neglected the life of the heart.

I recognize it is important that we do not live solely by our feelings, but we cannot discount the power of *experiencing* love. Many say love is not a feeling. There is truth to this, but it dismisses the emotional connection that love carries. I am not talking about lust or a burst of emotional ecstasy, but an emotional reference for love's power. One does not need a feeling to move towards love, but we do need an ability to connect to the power of love from the heart.

A CHAIN REACTION

When we live for decades without filling the needs of the heart, we become accustomed to the emptiness. We essentially become zombies with no heart connection to life. Our ability to connect to sadness as well as joy; grief as well as celebration, become lost. The heart is meant to experience all those facets of emotion. But if we don't allow our hearts to engage those areas, how can we develop a reference for a healthy heart? In order to make this a reality, two important keys need to be understood.

IT ALL BEGINS WITH THOUGHT

First, we need to understand that limiting beliefs and toxic thinking have negatively affected the life of our hearts. Areas of agreement, belief systems and our daily self-talk are based on thoughts that have come into our life. Our past experiences have an influence, but it's the interpretation of those events that impact us the most.

The thoughts that affect us the most involve the deep belief systems of how we see God, ourselves and others. What is in our heart will directly influence how we act, react and behave.

These toxic thoughts reveal very clearly that we are at war. This is not a physical conflict, nor is it against another human. We are surrounded by a spiritual battle over what we will believe. There is an enemy giving us thoughts that feel like they are our own. Daily and hourly, we are being bombarded with thoughts that could negatively affect our peace, health and sanity.

Satan's job is quite simple: give us thoughts that prevent the life of God from flowing to and through us. These thoughts become foundational belief systems that influence our entire life in a negative way. The enemy is incredibly diligent in this assault. One of his primary objectives is to prevent the work of love from filling our lives effectively.

What is he after? Our unresolved brokenness.

These unhealed areas of our heart give satan and his army room to flood us with toxic thinking. These feelings and perceptions either counterfeit love or fill us with patterns that make us avoid true love. We must learn to discern the *source* of our thoughts, to recognize the enemy's work.

You must see the resistance that prevents you from entering into daily love as the enemy's work and not just the way you are. He is the thief. It may feel like you, but IT IS NOT YOU. The thoughts may feel like your own, but they are the result of the enemy speaking to you. This is the enemy's attack, to perpetuate thoughts that keep you from loving yourself and others freely.

HEART HEALING

The second thing we must understand is our need for heart healing. I know that some reading this do not think they have a broken heart. Life seems manageable so they don't give the subject much thought. Brokenness is often not identified until severe levels of pain begin to manifest. When life seems to be falling apart, people are jolted into figuring out what to do.

What is needed is simple recognition to the issue that has been ignored for some time. I have found that helping people to understand they have a broken heart can be the first and most important stage in coaching them towards wholeness. They have often lived with a "get over it" attitude so intensely, they gave little room for weakness, grieving and healing. I'm often inclined to help them see the wound, so they can stop putting Band-Aids over emotional lacerations and contusions they have experienced. Once they can recognize it, there is often a deep sigh of relief, because I have just empowered them to address the deeper issues. Sometimes we just need permission to be vulnerable so that God can do a powerful work of restoration in our lives.

A broken heart starts with seeing where love has not been experienced. Wherever there is a lack of love, brokenness resides. Anyone who struggles with processing love needs healing in some area of the heart. The reason we become broken in the absence of love is because we were designed to carry love in every area of our life.

Anyone who doesn't admit to at least some struggle regarding the subject of love is either lying or in denial. We all need healing to some degree. Not only that, we need continual healing, because life has many challenges that pierce us. Healing to the heart is not just a one-time event, but a posture we maintain, where God always has access to touch the tender issues that affect our life.

You don't need to be a crying mess to recognize you need healing to your heart. Most who need the greatest healing don't feel anything at all. That's the problem—they don't feel! Their hearts have been shut down for a while and they carry little reference for the dynamic power of love. In order to move forward, recognition for heart healing is critical. Otherwise you are just wasting your time.

SPIRITUAL HEART DISEASE

Today, because of the lack of cultivating self-love, many wander through life with severe spiritual heart conditions. These arise when we do not address the pain we experience in life. As a child, our hearts are wide open to be loved and to experience the adventure of love. Yet over time, we can lose that childlike tenderness that embraces love with wonder and expectancy.

Severe spiritual heart conditions fester over time. There are six of them that I outline. If not addressed, the conditions worsen. Typically, people do not end up in my office until they are at the last condition. They have lived for years without cultivating a love relationship with God, themselves and others.

As you read through this section, if you feel you cannot relate to a certain stage, I ask you to revisit the previous one, for that is mostly likely where you are at. The good news is that wherever you are, there is hope for God to breathe change, if you are open.

1. A Broken Heart. This is where it all begins. Everyone on the planet has a broken heart, because we are all broken to some degree. No one has received love or given love perfectly. The quicker we can identify that we carry a broken heart, the quicker God can bring a greater revelation of love.

Self-love cannot be experienced when we leave a broken heart unattended. The broken heart is a condition that arises when those who were supposed to love us did not. They either released harmful actions against us or they neglected to act in loving ways that we needed.

Most people carry a broken heart because they were NOT given what they needed. This becomes difficult to identify unless we get a reference for what we did not have. For instance, the majority of people have no memory of their earthly father saying the words, "I love you." Yet without knowing this was a needed experience, people will live with little healing or resolution. They end up wounded but not knowing what they were missing.

2. Fearful Heart. Any area of brokenness makes room for fear to enter, leading us to not feeling secure in who we are and where we are headed. Insecurity is the land where fear loves to dwell. A heart filled with fear becomes trained to avoid any past pain from reoccurring.

Love has such a powerful effect that it will actually cast out fear[1]. Love and fear displace each other. When I am neck deep in fear, it drives out my ability to sense and experience the power of love. When I am living in the divine sense of knowing I am loved and allowing that love to settle within myself, fear has no ability to control my thoughts. The answer to fear is love, yet

---

[1] 1 John 4:18

every form of fear will pitch a fit to keep our hearts bound by its torment.

3. Angry Heart. As our fears remain intact, the stress and insecurity add another layer on top of fear; anger. The anger comes in to defend our brokenness and keep anyone away who may show a potential threat to us. All anger stems from unresolved brokenness and very little of it has anything to do with the current situation or subject. Most of the time, anger has way more to do with a past wound that has never been addressed.

So many attempt to use anger *management* as a solution. Yet that is all they end up doing—attempting to *manage* it. When in reality they should be removing this intruder. But we cannot remove something that we have allowed to become a defense mechanism.

An angry heart left unaddressed leaves a person with a lot of hostility within. The person may be angry with a past relationship, family member or life disappointment, but the target of their fury is often against themselves. They carry a pent up bitter world that drives the angry presence. The hostility may remain bottled up or it will lash out on others.

4. Hopeless Heart. When we walk through life overcompensating for our brokenness and serving our fears every day, we get exhausted. I know I did. We can only be angry for so long until we hit an exhaustion stage. Depression sets in. Energy levels are drained and irritability is high.

At this point, faith becomes worn out. The promises of God seem far away and breakthrough seems out of reach. Hope weakens as our minds become vulnerable to every negative thought that crosses the airwaves.

This is where people develop a "hope deferred" condition. *Hope deferred makes the heart sick[1]*. Hope that is delayed or lost can become a spiritual sickness that can even lead to physical sickness. Hope is a lifeline for our lives and when it seems distant, out of reach or delayed for too long, we suffer the effects of it. People at this stage have few tools for overcoming. Their lens on life carries a lot of negativity and cynicism, while a good future seems lost.

5. Hard Heart. When we fail to address the previous stages, we develop a dangerous condition called a hard heart. The heart has now lost its ability to believe because a callousness has formed. So even when a message of freedom is given to us, our eyes are veiled and hearing is dulled from receiving it.

Hard hearts are not open to hearing encouragement or hope anymore. I have found that it takes a divine work of the Holy Spirit and the person's willingness for a hard heart to be softened.

Wherever there is a hardened callousness in our hearts, we become more resistant to the transformative work of God. Areas that need change become stubborn. The only solution to a hard heart is the act of humbling ourselves before God as well as others. When we do this, we position our hearts for the hardness to melt off and tenderness to take residence.

6. Numb or Checked Out Heart. Getting to this stage is deadly. Of all the people I have worked with over the last 20 years, the numb and checked out heart has been one of the most

---

[1] Proverbs 13:12

challenging to help. When the heart is engaged, the possibilities are endless, but when it is not, there is very little others can do.

The deception of numbness can begin during seasons of intense pain. When someone hits this stage of numbness, they don't just become numb to a specific pain, they begin to become numb to everything. We are deceived when we think we can select what we numb out to.

One can minister a 100 tons of nuclear love from heaven, but a person can still sense nothing, because they are numbed out. There is very little engagement and heart connection. You can see it in their eyes. Lights are on but no one's home. Any attempts to address a key area of brokenness and they check out. They may be present in the room, but absent emotionally.

People at this stage have either given up tending to their heart or never did so to begin with. Those who have become weary with their hurt, pain, anger and fears can often slide into a place of numbness. The pain becomes so unbearable that "checking out" becomes a programmed way of living. They can go to work, pay their bills and say "thank you;" but inside, they are numb.

TURNING OFF THE MAIN BREAKER

When I help people in various stages of heart conditions, I coach them to never let their heart grow hard. Furthermore, I plead with them to never turn the heart off into numbness. Flipping the heart switch off hits the main power breaker inside. It affects everything and initiates a chain reaction to disconnect a person from relational connection. Very few announce this act publicly, but millions of people are quietly going numb.

In the Bible, David is the greatest example of keeping one's heart alive and continually engaging from the heart. He would cry out with prayers of desperation, while at times even wondering where God was in the midst of his circumstances. He rejoiced with all his might in victories and wept deeply during seasons of sorrow. The key was he was always heart engaged.

So I encourage people, if you're mad at God, go ahead and tell him. If you're sad, cry out to Him with everything you got. At some point in the heart exchange, God will meet you and lead you into transformation.

Without this adjustment, our culture will manifest what Jesus prophesied, *the love of many growing cold*[1]. We lose our ability to love ourselves, which then reflects on our relationships with others.

LOVING FROM A LOVED HEART

Before we go any further, it is imperative to engage your heart. Awaken it. Ask God to give you a new heart. Turn the heart switch back on. Humble yourself and allow the work of God to revive your heart. Face the pain you suppressed. Grieve through what you did not allow yourself to grieve. Let God once and for all breathe healing into your heart. Out of that will flow a chain reaction to everything else.

The good news is that you have a choice as to where your heart goes. So many will say, "Just follow your heart." But the

---

[1] Matthew 24:12

heart can be lured into dysfunctional trails. To resolve this, I have established the importance of leading my heart towards affections and meditations that keep me in the life of love.

The word often used for the love of God is the Greek word *agape*, which really speaks about the love of choice. It's an act of the will—a decision. When we walk into the great power of love, we actually make a decision. Today, you can choose to lead your heart into the depth of agape love. This is the kind of love that will change your life forever.

No one can make this choice for you. The following chapters will be meaningless if you do not engage your heart. My desire for you is to have an open heart exchange, whereby the Spirit of God can help you remove the blockage and toxicity in your heart and allow His healing power to set your heart free to love and be loved!

In our next chapter, I want to begin addressing the spiritual enemy that comes against you, keeping you from being able to experience the amazing depth of God's love for you, so you can love yourself and others.

QUESTIONS FOR CONSIDERATION

1. Take some time to ponder what it would mean to slow down and pay attention to the life of your heart. What do you need to do to pay more attention to the life of *your* heart?

2. How is your heart? How would you describe the condition of your heart right now? Take some time to write it down.

3. What do you want the life of your heart to experience?

4. Do you recognize the brokenness in your heart? In what ways can you let love come and heal those areas of your heart?

5. Describe a time where you were tempted to shut off your heart and numb out to life. What was that like? In what way would it be healthy to face that pain?

6. Which of the six spiritual heart conditions could you relate to the most? At what stage do you see yourself?

7. What is it going to take for you to walk in greater spiritual heart health? Write it down.

PRAYER

Father God, thank you for sending Jesus Christ to demonstrate your great love for me. Thank you that He came to release a ministry of healing to the broken hearted. I recognize that I have areas of my heart that have not been perfected in love. I humble myself before you today, so that you can perform spiritual heart surgery on my pain, emptiness and weaknesses. Forgive me for not tending to my heart or for ignoring issues of the heart. I need you to teach me how to watch over and process life through my heart. I want to learn to experience love in the fullest, so I position my heart to grow in love. Let my interactions with You and others help me experience the power that love brings. I receive love, because I know You are love, Father. In Jesus name, amen.

03

The War Over Self-Love

You can't fight a battle you don't think exists.
— John Eldredge, *Wild at Heart*

I cannot afford to have a thought in my head about me that is not in His.
— Bill Johnson

Ask anyone about their relationships and you will quickly find tension and challenges. Why is something so amazing as love so difficult? Why do we spend most of our days jumping over relational hurdles and recovering from tainted experiences? Isn't there a much better way to live?

Before we get to *why* love can be so challenging, it's important to note that God created relationships to be the incubator where love gets formed in our lives. Visible human interactions are designed to help us understand the invisible God. The tension in our relationships identifies where love is calling for a deeper work. It also reveals the spiritual conflict over loved being experienced from our Father in heaven.

God is a God of love. In fact, He *is* love. He doesn't just have love; He *is* the very essence of love. Whenever you interact with love in its truest form, you are coming into contact with the nature of the Father.

If we interact with God and do not experience loving connection, something is getting in the way or we are engaging a false-god. Millions of people in history have actually missed the God of creation, the great Heavenly Father, because they have not interacted with His deepest nature as love. He IS love!

Keep in mind, there is an enemy to God's character being manifested in the earth. Satan is busy building a resistance to what God has created. We must become illuminated to the all-out war over love being received and given out. Whether we acknowledge it, believe it or deny it, the war is very real and near to our lives.

The enemy want nothing less than to steal, kill and destroy our ability to flow in love. He wants to separate us in every way possible from receiving God's love, loving ourselves and giving it away. His playbook is filled with assaults that are thrown against our life, our families and our generations—all to keep us from the freeing power of love.

Why does it seem that every novel, movie and play production depict struggles in relationships? Because that is the narrative of our daily life. John and Staci Eldredge, in their book Love and War, say, "*We live in a great love story, set in the midst of war.*[1]" We are surrounded by an invisible battlefield that wrestles over our ability to walk in the fullness of love relationship. Our enemy knows if he can compromise our lens of love, then everything else is simply details.

---

[1] Eldridge, John and Staci. *Love and War: Find Your Way to Something Beautiful in Your Marriage.* Colorado Springs: WaterBrook, 2011

We do not wrestle with other human beings, even though we often view people as the enemy target. The battle is not even with ourselves, as most have been trained to think. *The first thing you need to know is the battle is an invisible war against you.* If you see your love struggles as just "you", then you will feel defeated and fall under toxic thoughts every time. You must see it as an outside resistance manifesting in you and not just your own thoughts.

You cannot see the spiritual enemy to God's love, but you can feel the effects of the battle, by checking the thoughts that come against you. If you are good at identifying negative emotions, you can probably discern the interference in your mind. Pay attention to the emotions and struggles you battle and you will hear the enemy's voice. The impressions that lock you down from love are not your own, but a system designed to isolate you from love.

Allow your eyes to see the war, but let me warn you ahead of time; once you get a glimpse of this conflict, there is no turning back. Like Neo in the Matrix, observing the grid of warfare leaves us no choice but to break free and help others shake off the chains. The moment you learn to love and accept yourself as God's child, it's game over for the enemy and he knows it. I believe that all we need is to become aware of the resistance and gain the right tools to win the battle.

SEPARATED FROM LOVE

One of the most challenging emotions to experience is that of separation in relationship. Most of us can understand that feeling separated from God or any treasured person can trigger great pain and even emotional torment. This is because you and I were made to live in the safety of connection.

Satan is the author of perpetuating relational separation. Because he has been eternally separated from intimacy with God, he wants to place his personal torment upon you. He frantically seeks to cultivate all forms of lies to make you feel relationally disconnected. I believe that he actually spends the majority of his resources assaulting people in this manner.

If he blocks the experience of love from the heart, a person will suffer under the pain that the feelings of separation bring. The mind will struggle to maintain fruitful thinking. The health of the body can erode and relationships will suffer. The enemy knows, all he has to do is mess with the love factor and he can take you out.

But when you truly encounter love from the Father, you are a life-giving weapon of power to dismantle the enemy in your world. Love is the conduit by which all life-change occurs. It will drive fear out of someone's life. Love will unleash a healing salve to our brokenness and calm our inward storms. Love is the answer, so do not be surprised when love is warred against in your life.

WHAT IS EMPTY SEEKS TO BE FILLED

When self-love has been absent from our hearts, we are left with a tragic emptiness. Unfortunately, a person can become so used to the absence of love, they never realize what the heart is missing. I lived for many years lacking self-love, but also never realizing I even needed it.

Over time, you and I will search for answers to fill the empty spaces in our hearts. We begin to crave counterfeit experiences that never satisfy. Meanwhile our hearts will develop a resistance towards true love settling in.

Without a healthy reference, pure love can be seen as smog rather than clean air. Receiving a compliment, a hug or someone seeing our flaws can be so incredibly painful when self-love is absent. As a result, most people run away from intimate connection rather than embracing it safely.

This resistance that forms is what keeps us from healing and moving forward. A stream of dysfunctional thinking forms to keep us in bondage. It is important that we expose the thoughts that keep us from love so we can take our peace back. The voices that keep us bound need to be revealed as a bunch of lies for they can only be displaced with authentic love.

EARLY SIGNS OF ATTACK

The resistance to self-love can begin its work very early in our lives. Most have it in their generations as it forms the family dynamics very early on. It's easy to become accustomed to the voices and the emotional dysfunction, never seeing that anything is wrong.

The resistance shows up within your inner dialogue, telling you how ugly you look, how unqualified you are; pouncing on your every insecurity, keeping you in a prison where you cannot freely love yourself. It jumps up when someone attempts to love on you. It keeps people at a distance and isolates you in a prison of self vs self-battles.

The voice gives you an altered perception when you look in the mirror. It doesn't let you post a selfie on Facebook because it magnifies certain features negatively and creates an unpleasant perception of your image. This resistance kicks up when someone hugs you, keeping you uncomfortable with affection. It causes you to hide in your own shadow because it has trained you to not feel safe in your own skin.

Many authors communicate the cry of humanity in how we struggle to love ourselves. The well-known actress, Amy Poehler wrote a book entitled "Yes Please," where she sums up her childhood struggles and the self-hating voice she listened to. Watch her words as she articulates the battle that so many of us face when it comes to how we see ourselves.

That voice that talks badly to you is a demon voice. This very patient and determined demon shows up in your bedroom one day and refuses to leave. You are six or twelve or fifteen and you look in the mirror and you hear a voice so awful and mean that it takes your breath away. It tells you that you are fat and ugly and you don't deserve love. And the scary part is the demon is your own voice. But it doesn't sound like you. It sounds like a strangled and seductive version of you. Think Darth Vader or an angry Lauren Bacall. The good news is there are ways to make it stop talking. The bad news is it never goes away. If you are lucky, you can live a life where the demon is generally forgotten, relegated to a back shelf in a closet next to your old field hockey equipment. You may even have days or years when you think the demon is gone. But it is not. It is sitting very quietly, waiting for you . . .

And then one day, you go through a breakup or you can't lose your baby weight or you look at your reflection in a soupspoon and that slimy bugger is back. It moves its sour mouth up to your ear and reminds you that you are fat and ugly and don't deserve love.[1]

For me, the voice told me my legs looked stupid and I walked funny. My knees kind of hit each other as I walked and that inner voice directed all my attention to this. I didn't know the enemy was speaking to me, so I just obeyed it by constantly paying attention to those self-hating thoughts. I spent hours of my childhood standing in front of the mirror, trying to find ways to walk so that my legs would not appear so "knock-kneed."

I practiced walking over and over; hoping people would not see the goofiness I was so obsessed over. No one ever really said anything to me, but it didn't matter. I was beating myself up in my thoughts every day. What I didn't realize was that another voice was speaking, sounding like my own; baiting me to come into agreement and make those thoughts my own. Unfortunately, I allowed this to carry on for a long time.

These self-rejecting thoughts pointed out that my head was too big and my eyes were not the right size. I was chubby as a kid for various reasons, so I would obsess over my belly and pudgy midsection. My peers added to the insecurity; pointing out my belly and calling me names. I allowed the voice to tell me I looked ugly and that being overweight was appalling to people.

During my junior high years, I was in the midst of pubescent transitions. Like many other adolescents, that season was

---

[1] Poehler, Amy. Yes Please (Kindle Locations 324-335). HarperCollins. Kindle Edition.

incredibly awkward for me. At a summer camp, a bunch of friends I had met all gathered by the pool to enjoy a hot day of swimming. One girl motioned to the guys to jump in the pool and each boy took their shirt off before jumping in. As soon as I removed mine, she took one look at me and shook her head in disappointment. "Go ahead and put yours back on," she said with dead panned eyes and a smirk of cynicism. The pain of those words remained with me for decades.

I covered up all this self-hating pain by being funny. I would rank on others before they could expose me. Quite often, my teasing got out of hand, as I hit nerves that were raw for people. I regret how I coped with my pain by hurting others. Through jokes, I shamed others with the same shame I experienced. I made fun of an overweight kid or put someone in a hot seat of comedic lines to keep anyone from throwing it at me. It was my only way to survive in this emotional jungle I lived in.

God has healed me of so much of it, but I just wish back in those days I had someone tell me these thoughts were not my own and I could get free of them. I also wish someone told me I was handsome.

A lack of self-love makes us uncomfortable with affection. We end up struggling to receive compliments and affirmation from others. Intimacy and connection does not come easily, as fear and numbness get in the way. People without self-love can jump into lust filled experiences, but struggle to feel comfortable with true intimacy.

Not loving myself conditioned me to become my own worst enemy. I developed perfectionistic tendencies with the hopes I would feel safe and loved. No one was harder on me than I was on myself. I considered it an admirable trait, not realizing I was actually damaging myself.

How many do the very same thing today? They fail to grant themselves grace and kindness; always getting so stressed and angry over so much that goes on in life. Growing up, many people never saw their lack of self-love tendencies. They were able to live so long with their false coping skills, their issues remained hidden under the surface.

Many high level achievers and prolific performers have deep self-hatred issues that keep destructive tendencies in their life. They can hide behind fame and results, but deep down inside, their relational capacity is void. In ministering to countless people over the decades, I have observed that even the most prominent of personalities you see in media can actually be very shallow people up close. They have the ability to perform, but very little depth in relational connectivity.

UNLOVING MINDSETS

A lack of self-love produces a very unloving mindset in our lives. Typically, when we hear the word unloving, we think of someone doing something unkind or cruel towards another. Yet the meaning of the word can travel much deeper. When looking at *unloving* tendencies, we are actually speaking of not giving or reciprocating affection, being coldhearted or lacking in the ability to have sympathy or to feel love.[1]

In the New Testament Scriptures, *unloving* speaks to an

---

[1] http://www.thefreedictionary.com/unloving

inability to process natural affection. The Greek word "storgē" is translated in English as "love" but in the context of affection. Love carries an exchange of affection, which is established first in our relationship with our parents and is intended to grow as we mature.

In the Scriptures, the word "storgē" is used in a negative context; "a-storgē," which means "without natural affection." When we live without reference for natural affection, this void opens us up to all sorts of relational struggles.

The book of Romans[1] and 2 Timothy[2] both give warnings as to an impending spiritual decline in society. Their words prophesy what will manifest as people remove themselves from the God of love to follow after counterfeit desires. The word "unloving" is listed amongst all the other destructive manifestations.

In the days ahead, more people will be conditioned to live without the power of pure love; its absence becoming a way of life. As the struggle increases, masses will chase after counterfeit affections. Most will look to addictions; others will be drawn away by unfulfilling distractions. Many will simply grow cold and check out.

The problem goes back to our history with affection and whether or not we have healthy references for it. Unloving patterns arise when we lack the ability to give and receive pure affection in our relationships. The void conditions us to isolate from healthy connection and draws us into dysfunctional

---

[1] Romans 1:28-31

[2] 2 Timothy 3:3-6

patterns.

At the time of this writing, I was curiously listening to a well-known comedian being interviewed on the radio. I am fascinated with discovering what motivates people and drives their decisions in life. In this particular interview, I listened as a female comedian shared that she has not been in a committed relationship for a while. The interviewer quickly assumed she had not been sexually active, asking how she had been able to deal with that.

Without hesitation and absolute candor, the comedian exclaimed, "Oh I just had sex this weekend; a bunch of times as a matter of fact. With someone I know. There's nothing more, I just need to be able to do that sometimes." Even the liberal interviewer was stunned at this shallow response.

Most celebrities don't see the need to be married to have sex, but even further, this woman didn't even see the need to be emotionally connected to have sexual intercourse! This is a high level manifestation of a lack of self-love in operation.

Most of the people who come to me have a level of love deficiency in their life. They often make an appointment for personal coaching when the problem is at DEFCON levels. Rarely do people see the warning signs early enough where they can make simple modifications. At this stage, they are a mental wreck, their bodies are in need of desperate healing or they are checked out emotionally, showing they actually gave up years ago. They expect me to give them instant fixes from decades of not being love properly. The solution is love, but they can be scared to death of experiencing it. Embracing true love is incredibly challenging for someone who has not loved themselves for a long time.

This creates a culture that is unfamiliar with the love of God. This is what Jesus warned of when He said in the last days, *the love of many will grow cold.*

And because lawlessness will abound, the love of many will grow cold. Matthew 24:12

Lawlessness, as referenced in this verse, involves a lack of moral restraint that keeps us from falling into darkness and destructive behaviors. The lawlessness we will witness has a lot to do with hearts not being healed, causing love to become more absent.

When the love of many grows cold, it's a dangerous climate to live in. All manner of fights, strife and contentions erupt when love is not present. Our relationships become accusatory, nit-picky and offense ridden. Over time people harden themselves to the beauty of tender love.

The answer to this dilemma is pure love flowing from God through our interactions. In loving relationship, God is given room to transform our lives and enhance our identities. The resistance seeks to keeps us from God's love, so that we cannot sense an all-loving God throughout the day. In fact, the enemy wants us to believe that God is not even loving to begin with.

A MASSIVE EMPTINESS

The trail to our relational struggles stems back to our ability to live in the power of love, especially in how well we love ourselves. Love is so vital that our entire lives can crumble in its absence. Our ability to love ourselves and others is what fruitfulness in life hinges on. So when the connection to love is compromised, every manner of struggles can invade a person's life.

When love is present, life is simple and uncluttered. When love is compromised to any degree, spider webs of struggle form and spread rapidly, making relationships complicated and energy sapping. That is why the majority of all transformative work must be built on restoring pure love in the hearts of mankind. Every manner of deception, bondage and torment has some form of compromised love in its root system.

The resistance to self-love does not discriminate, for we can find its menacing work in any culture, demographic and social setting. For those who have not been loved and trained to love themselves properly, four main enemy mindsets seek to fill the void. They involve, fear, self-rejection, self-condemnation and anger.

The very basis of self-love involves total self-acceptance, with no string attached. Acceptance grants us value from simply *being* and not from doing, therefore driving out any need to perform or strive. When we give ourselves complete self-acceptance, we gain the power to grow at light speed. Without it, we subtly reject and even abhor our personal flaws, weaknesses and mistakes.

A large percentage of those I have helped live with self-rejecting mindsets on a regular basis. They are not aware of it at first, because they have a poor sense of self-love. No examples of self-acceptance have been put before them.

Because of this chasm, self-rejection becomes commonplace. Our interactions fill up with exchanges that devalue who we are. We engage life from a position that is so far beneath how precious we are. Most people self-deprecate before anyone else has the chance to, because we are so aware of our flaws more than we are connected to our true worth.

Because we often self-reject, we never enter into the depth that relationships can offer. I wasn't able to receive a compliment or look at someone in the eye who was genuinely connecting to me. I avoided deeper social settings because my self-rejection would be exposed. On top of that, people often loved me more than I loved myself.

When we are insecure about ourselves, we become prone to fear in relationships. This blocks us from resting in the power that love carries. We all want love, but we run from it because fear trains us to avoid any relational hurt. Our past pain becomes stamped with fear, keeping us from taking risks and engaging true intimacy. The torment of fear gains leverage in the absence of love, especially because genuine self-love is unfamiliar for so many.

When we live in fear, vulnerability feels like frightening exposure, rather than an opportunity for authentic connection. If we cannot experience love for ourselves, then fear will have a dominant voice and presence. That is why the Scriptures teach that the very presence of love actually casts out the work of fear[1]. When we are afraid, it's not a courage issue, but a love deficiency. Love is the solution, but fear seeks to block us from it.

To heal my self-love struggles, I also had to confront the anger I carried inside. I have found this to be true in all those I have helped as well. This anger is not typically an outward manifestation, but an inward hostility. The anger lives under the surface and causes a pent up tension.

This anger conditions us to be hard on ourselves. The greatest toll on a person's life is the self-condemnation they carry. Think about it, when a relationship lacks love, the interactions quickly become accusatory and full of blame. The same is true when we do not love ourselves. Our inner world becomes flooded with self-blame, guilt and accusing thoughts. Those who lack healthy love for themselves have very black and white thinking, never giving themselves room to grow or overcome failures.

I often find that those with heavy religious upbringings were not immersed in the power of love and acceptance. Their spiritual grid was filled with perfectionism and performance; therefore, condemnation was their lens for life. Self-condemning

---

[1] 1 John 4:18

thoughts keeps an accusing voice in your head, where you live in criticism of yourself. You can also become critical of others who should love you, but cannot. Constant arguments go on within, never allowing a person to be settled in the peace that loving yourself brings.

The enemy brings a resistance to everything that God's love seeks to establish in your life. This keeps you from seeing the value that is inside you, the power within you and the beauty that you possess. The resistance completely opposes what God's Word says about who you are and what you are capable of.

Most families who have these self-love struggles conduct their home under its influence. These anti-love patterns literally become a familiar dysfunction in the generations. Unless families gain a biblical grid for health, they won't know how to destroy the insidious patterns that lurk within the root system of the family tree.

Parents who do not raise their children in healthy love and affection can set them up to have a poor sense of identity and an empty reference to what self-love needs to be. Our hurtful experiences and painful traumas can reinforce a poor image of ourselves and create a distance to the power of love.

It's also important to know that true love includes healthy discipline and correction. Without it, we do not understand the fullness of love nor what it means to live in true family connection. Many children who were not corrected and disciplined in their home properly can grow up with deep struggles in healthy relationships. Their definition of self-love can look more like selfishness and entitlement.

The absence of love keeps millions locked in a prison of inner conflict. It leaves us questioning our identity and living in constant double-mindedness. Many who have this at work do not know who they are and continually struggle with confusion and disorientation.

With no reference for self-love, we live with a veil over our eyes, where receiving love from God and others is challenging. Survival tools kick in to further reinforce the prison and fear will keep us from breaking out into freedom.

Receiving true love is the key to destroying this problem, yet millions are seeking for something they have no reference for. It's so much easier to accept the counterfeits that come our way.

To break through this resistance, we first need to clear away a key wall that prevents us from dealing with any of our issues. I have found there to be little success in setting people free unless we remove this toxic factor from our lives. We will address this in our next chapter.

QUESTIONS FOR CONSIDERATION

1. When you interact with God, do you automatically feel loved by Him? If not, what factors do you think contributed to this?

2. Have you ever felt separated from God? Like He is far away? Why do you think so many battle this issue so much?

3. When you think about self-love struggles, what personal battles come to mind?

4. Can you remember in childhood how struggles with self-love began to arise? Take a moment to write down or share that early experience.

5. What specific resistance do you need to face to move more into loving yourself?

PRAYER

Father God, I acknowledge today that you are a God of love. You do not just have love, You are love. I position myself to receive who You are. Thank you for being love and for loving me. I recognize today that You love, because that is who You are.

I am beginning to recognize there are some patterns that have come into my life that do not want me to experience the fullness of Your love. I ask that you open the eyes of my understanding, so that I may remove any hindering mindsets from my life. I want to love and be loved fully as Your child. I ask that ways of thinking, believing and living that keep me from love be exposed in my life and dismantled, in Jesus name, amen.

04

The Game of Shame

there is no fear in love . . .
1 John 4:18

Neither do I condemn you; go and sin no more.
John 8:11

There is no love without relationship.

Powerful relationships do not exist without intimacy.

Yet we cannot experience intimacy unless we become vulnerable.

For many, *vulnerability* is a very scary word. You may have even squirmed after reading it.

The truth is, we cannot have the great relationships we want unless we open our hearts, let our guards down and let our true selves be seen. Vulnerability allows the vast spectrum of who we are to be processed amongst safe people.

Yet the majority of society lives closed off to vulnerable and authentic relationships. We all seem to have our walls, coping mechanisms and methods for dodging uncomfortable subjects.

No wonder we are exhausted and frustrated. Our lives do not have the loving environment that we can rest and heal in.

I can remember sharing personal struggles with other men and experiencing responses that made me regret even opening up. My intentions were to connect and grow through authentic sharing. I vividly remember the disappointment and humiliation I felt from receiving the most uncomfortable responses. I'm sure you've been there.

Those moments of feeling rejected, getting the blank stare, hearing a "sermon-like" reply or receiving some Christian cliché make us curl up into a cocoon and wish we were invisible. Those reactions are beyond painful. Relationships become so hard when people do not know how to authentically share and express safe vulnerability.

A lack of self-love has taught us to accept core relationships that are less than fulfilling. Our exchanges, therefore, maintain a surface-level interaction. Our capacity to deal with brokenness and struggle is incredibly low, yet our use of protective coping mechanisms is at an all-time high.

We dodge each other instead of safely connecting. We leave relationships just before there's a chance to break through into deeper intimacy. In my work helping people, I am grieved at how many are unable to address their brokenness in a down to earth manner. Way too many are attempting to survive with defensive behavior; seeking to preserve whatever reputation or persona they can.

Families often struggle to process through brokenness and struggles in day to day life. A lack of spiritual and emotional safety keeps members of the home from working through their battles. If people do not feel safe, then healthy sharing will rarely occur. As a result, many will remain silent in their torment and never experience the power of healing that authentic vulnerability can bring.

John Eldredge articulates this modern plague with great accuracy. His words describe the daily tension that wars in people over connecting authentically with one another.

> *Notice how we are in elevators: No one makes eye contact. No one wants to acknowledge that we are seeing and being seen. In a moment of forced intimacy, almost claustrophobic intimacy, we pretend we aren't even there.*
>
> *The reason? Most times we just don't know what to do with what we see. About ourselves, I mean.*
>
> *It doesn't take a Nobel Prize winner to know that something dreadful has happened to the human race. So we stare at the ceiling or our shoes; we watch the numbers report the passing floors; we hide. This is how most of us approach our entire lives—we hide what we can, work on what we feel is redeemable, and despise the rest.*[1]

THE ENEMY OF INTIMACY

We are all dying to connect, but at the same time we avoid intimacy like a plague. It is incredibly dysfunctional, but unfortunately it is how we live.

---

[1] John Eldridge *The Utter Relief of Holiness*

What keeps us in this perpetual hide and seek from God? Why do we constantly cover our true selves from each other?

We mourn that our lives lack intimate relationships, but we act goofy when the opportunity for connection arises.

What drives all this relational insanity?

The answer is one word. *Shame.*

It has been in play ever since Adam and Eve's fall. The moment sin entered the planet, shame came along to separate us from the very thing we needed in our brokenness—intimacy. Whenever we feel flawed, shame conditions us to withdraw and hide, preventing us from landing in safe connection. Ironically, we run from the very thing we need in order to be set free from our bondage.

When it comes to brokenness, shame gets on the front lines of attack to prevents us from taking any steps to get free. Shame keeps us in a prison of isolation, so the issues of the heart cannot be healed in the love of God.

Without shame in the picture, dealing with any personal struggle is so much easier. Mistakes, bad decisions and sinful choices can be faced and healed in the light of love. Yet too many of our interactions are shame-based. Therefore, our lives become so complicated and even filled with drama.

Let's be honest, other people don't always create safe environments for healing. Their lack of being healed themselves shows they don't know how to keep shame out. Therefore, most people remain in their patterns. Shame has conditioned us to hide and cover up.

SHAME IN THE BEGINNING

At the dawn of creation, mankind lived in the relational openness we were designed to possess. Adam and Eve walked naked without any shame. They openly connected to God and each other with no need to cover up.

There wasn't even a need for clothing, as awkward as that sounds. Adam and Eve were clothed and covered by the glory of God. Interactions with the Creator were experienced freely, without interference or complications. At this time, connection with each other was unhindered.

God created us to connect openly with absolute freedom. When we cannot do this effectively, it is because something is interfering. Sin gave access for satan to throw a shame blanket over us so that we would lose the power that intimate connection provides.

And the eyes of them both were opened, and they knew that they were naked; and they sewed fig leaves together, and made themselves aprons. Genesis 3:7

Once Adam and Eve sinned, immediately their self-perception changed. Their thoughts were flooded with feelings they had never dealt with before. Impressions of uncleanness and fear entered to condemn their nakedness and accuse them. Shame convinced them to rectify the situation by covering themselves. They immediately ran in fear to hide from the voice and presence of their Lord.

Shame causes two main actions in our lives. **It first drives us in fear to avoid vulnerability.** The fear of exposure and the fear of rejection train us to put up walls of protection. In the biblical account, Adam and Eve ran away and hid.

The second thing shame does is train us to find coverings of our own. God designed us to be covered by love from God and those around us. Shame trains us to fear and avoid that at all costs. We try to behave better and attempt more religious acts to hopefully outweigh our inner feelings of shame.

And they heard the voice of the LORD God walking in the garden in the cool of the day: and Adam and his wife hid themselves from the presence of the LORD God amongst the trees of the garden. Genesis 3:8

Notice the very sound of the Lord walking in the garden freaked them out and triggered shame. It trained them to believe that God was furious and would beat them to a bloody pulp. Were there consequences for their actions? Certainly. But look at what God's first response is towards their sin.

Then the Lord God called to Adam and said to him, "Where are you?" Genesis 3:9

Did God *know* that Adam and Eve sinned?

Of course He did. He wasn't looking for an answer to a question that He already knew. He was showing us His heart.

Even in the midst of sin, God calls out with an invitation for relationship.

He surely could have vaporized Adam and Eve for disobeying the one command He gave them. Instead, He called out for His two most precious creations on the planet to draw near.

God has been doing that with mankind ever since. Yet satan has trained us to hide in shame from God and from each other.

Listen to Adam's response.

"I heard Your voice in the garden, and I was afraid because I was naked; and I hid myself." Genesis 3:10

Adam allowed shame and fear to become *one* with him in his thinking. He basically says, "I AM afraid" or "I AM fear." With no discernment regarding his feelings, Adam assumes this is now who he is. He had no idea an enemy was giving him these impressions to further separate him in his relationship with God.

Notice God's response.

And He said, "<u>Who told you</u> that you were naked? Have you eaten from the tree of which I commanded you that you should not eat?" Genesis 3:11

The "who told you" shows us that all the toxic thoughts and yucky feelings Adam had were not his own. Someone told him to feel the way he felt. In this case, the enemy had an open door to speak the thoughts and impressions Adam was feeling.

The same is true for you and I. Amidst our shame, fear and struggles to love ourselves, we have to ask, "who told me to think and feel this way?"

That someone can be a parent or a friend. But usually it is often the enemy speaking in our thoughts. It's satan's way of pushing us away from intimate relationship.

God longs for you and I to stand in the light and connect with Him and each other in love. Yet shame keeps us from ever being in that position, fearing we will be rejected, abandoned or banished. Our Father seeks to restore us from a shame mindset to a grace and love mindset, where we can be naked and without shame in relationship.

Only in open and loving relationship can you and I be healed and restored. The best way I can love myself and let others love me is to begin moving out of the shame games I play so that I can truly connect. If I remain in shame, I wall myself off from the healing available on the other side.

SHAME AND SELF-LOVE STRUGGLES

To overcome our self-love struggles, we have to unwind the conditioning of shame, because it prevents vulnerability. In Adam and Eve's case, they go from not even questioning their nakedness to immediate shame and inadequacy. Nothing is mentioned in the Scriptures about their bodies changing. All that changed was their perception.

I am not advocating that nakedness should have remained a norm. I am simply exposing the thought system that drives us to hide. I do think the attack on their nakedness has trickled down the generations, even to how mankind views their bodies. Humans are harder on their looks than ever. Can you see the spiritual assault on our self-image?

More and more people struggle with body image and an unhealthy relationship with food. Ironically, the whole shame battle entered over a temptation to eat. No wonder food and body image issues are so rampant.

God loves us perfectly, yet millions wrestle with experiencing it, because they have a shame-based foundation. Everyone around a person could love with a perfect love, but it wouldn't matter, they will run from it. Some develop a "shady" lifestyle or just avoid any depth when it comes to healthy relationship. Fear will drive their decisions, keeping them away from their fellow man and from God.

SHAME AND BLAME

One of the first signs that we carry shame in our lives is that we begin to blame. Shame carries an accusing voice against ourselves, which often leads us to accuse others.

Notice Adam's response to God's "who told you?" question.

Then the man said, "The woman whom You gave to be with me, she gave me of the tree, and I ate." Genesis 3:12

Shame makes us feel accused off the jump. If we listen to its voice, we can react by immediately blaming others, usually those closest to us. Adam blames his wife. *It's the woman's fault!*

His job was to cover Eve and watch over the garden. As Eve's covering, it was Adam's job to cast out the deceiver and keep the garden pure. Yet he did not fulfill his responsibility and he knew it.

Because of his shame mindset, Adam could not take responsibility for his lack of covering his wife. Eve was deceived, but Adam was responsible for relaying God's commands and implementing what He said. He let Eve walk right into this deception[1].

When men are filled with shame, they are often tempted to blame the woman; our wives, our mothers or women in general. As a man, this is hard for me to admit, but it's true.

---

[1] 1 Timothy 2:14, Romans 5:12

When a man feels shame it's because he feels like a failure. Mistakes become indictments to his identity. We feel accused in our thoughts of being incompetent; a man's worst nightmare.

Instead of recognizing the mistake and growing, a man is tempted to blame someone. If it's not the woman, it's his job, bosses, the economy or the president. He quietly blames himself in self-condemnation as this is the game shame plays on us.

Adam blames the woman and then blames God. *It's the woman YOU gave me!*

Shame trains us to feel accused, then point our accusation on God. *God, how could you do this? How could you allow this? Why did you put me in this marriage? Why did you give me this family? Why are you leaving me hanging?*

Once we begin to accuse God, we put ourselves in a perilous position, because in questioning the source of healing, we distance ourselves from connection with God. Shame doesn't even allow us to see God properly, because we end up questioning His goodness.

We've all done it. We come into agreement with satan's lies that God is not a good Father and therefore needs to be blamed for our situations. We feel He has left us hanging and He was the cause of the calamity.

Mankind does this over and over. We listen to lies of the enemy. We live them out. The enemy makes us feel terrible for what we did. He then convinces us to blame God for the whole thing. And the cycle continues.

Our Lord is inviting Adam into relationship, so he can take responsibility for his sin and grow. Yet Adam is hiding, covering himself and blaming everyone else.

Shame has taught you and I to do the same thing over and over again.

DISCERNING SHAME

There are many ways that we can define shame and observe the manifestations of it. Brené Brown, a leading researcher on the subject, defines it as *the intensely painful feeling or experience of believing that we are flawed and therefore unworthy of love and belonging.*[1]

Shame messes with our sense of belonging by emphasizing our flaws and highlighting our sins, leading us to feel unworthy. We begin to feel disqualified. Shame conditions our shoulders to sag, our heads to face the ground, our eyes to dart and our voices to mumble. We lack confidence because shame has convinced us we are not good enough. When we share our vulnerabilities, yet receive an unloving response, shame shuts us off from ever sharing again.

Growing up, difficult subjects were hard to talk about. Discussing boys, girls, puberty, sex or insecurities were such awkward subjects in our homes. So many of us were shamed when attempts were made to open up. The response of others communicated to us that what we were sharing was stupid or insignificant.

Oh just stop it.

Just get over it.

---

[1] http://brenebrown.com/2013/01/14/2013114shame-v-guilt-html/

Why are you making a big deal over that?

You struggle with what?

I've never struggled with that. That's weird.

All these words stirred up humiliation that caused many to hide in an abyss of isolation. Our parents and their generations hid their flaws and sins. Shame taught them to ignore those areas and close them away in secret closets. Anytime a family member tried to discuss these subjects, the person was chastised and depicted as crazy, so as to never bring up the issue again.

The more people do not talk about their struggles or the subject of shame, the more they actually have shame. In fact, darkness empowers shame's effects. The more we cover up the areas that need healing, the more powerful they become in destroying families and tearing down relational potential. We often think that if we hide them, we will preserve the family. Yet all we are left with is superficial family gatherings with no depth or life-change.

I have worked with a litany of families that were marked with shame patterns for generations. I've helped marriages and families address the shame issues that drive them to lie, cover up mistakes and hide any display of weakness. Shame thinking trickles down in families. Parents wonder why their children lie all the time or why dysfunctional patterns seem to remain. Shame keeps people from becoming vulnerable and getting the help needed to change.

I have winced in pain too many times when attempting to share a personal struggle with someone who did not have a shame-free response. Just by their body language alone, I could tell they didn't know how to deal with what I expressed. I wanted to crawl into a hole, regretting I ever brought up the subject. Responses like, "Really? I don't struggle with that" or "man, that's odd" made me first feel like absolute garbage. I immediately wanted to punch them in the face. How can we be so relationally awkward?

It's because people haven't dealt with the shame regarding their own issues. So many Christians live in hiding but they spiritualize it, saying, "It's all under the blood Mark." My response is often, "well then you should have no problem talking about it." If it's under the blood of Jesus, then the issue has been exposed in the light of God and we can talk about the healing you experienced. Problem is, their cliché statements are a cover up. Nothing is under the blood if it's hidden under the carpet.

WHAT SHAME DOES

There are a number of subtle, yet deadly things that shame perpetuates to keep us from healing our wounds and living in the safety of God's love.

Shame trains us to see ourselves as one with our sins and struggles. You may have sin, but you are not sin. You may have a struggle, but you are not a struggle. Shame will not only tell you that you did something bad, it will communicate that you *are* something bad. It is very accusatory and condemning in nature. Shame's goal is for you to see yourself through an unclean lens, where all you see is your mistakes and sins.

If this is not healed, we can often project our shame onto others. Those who shame others have a great deal of shame regarding themselves. They judge and dismiss people at the drop of the hat. Deep down inside, they are filled with the very same issues.

Shame drives us in fear to hide, rather than press in deeper to take risks of vulnerability. No relationship can grow without becoming honest and vulnerable. Shame keeps us from ever trying.

Shame teaches us to lie. Whenever you witness a pattern of lying taking place, fear and shame are a predominant presence. We lie because we fear being exposed and rejected. Shame teaches us to do whatever it takes to avoid being exposed. It will therefore justify any behavior needed to cover up.

We develop a defensive posture when we have shame. Why? Because we are trained to protect ourselves, rather than walk freely without that pressure to defend.

Shame keeps us from taking responsibility for our lives. With a shame-based mindset, taking responsibility means we blame ourselves with contempt. Yet taking responsibility does not have to be done in a way were we feel demeaned or stamped as a failure. The problem is that shame creates a distance from people realizing they need to take responsibility for their life and choices.

Shame keeps us from ever getting healed or free. God never shames us. Yet He asks that we come into the light so He can transform us in the atmosphere of connection with Him. Shame lies to us, convincing us that the light of God is scary. When in reality, God's light is warm and full of love. I find too many are deceived, thinking they can get free by themselves, without the help of others and without the act of coming clean in the light of God.

But if we walk in the light as He is in the light, we have fellowship with one another, and the blood of Jesus Christ His Son cleanses us from all sin. 1 John 1:7

I am amazed at the people that look for personal help, but do not want to come into the light. Their past is filled with deception and cover ups. They want freedom from their past, but they only want to get free while hiding.

The moment I let them know they may need to talk to the person they have hurt by their lies or choices, they back down and discontinue receiving help. No matter how kindly I suggest it, they recoil in defensiveness. They would rather live in darkness than come into the light.

People with shame use shame on others. Even the statement "shame on you" shows our alliance with shame in how we attempt to motivate others. No one will manifest long-term change when shame is used. We may witness a short-lived burst, but nothing of lasting fruit.

OVERCOMING THE SHAME RESPONSE

To love yourself and others freely, we have to get the shame lens off. When Jesus talked to people who were in the depths of sin, He never shamed them, but released a powerful invitation for people to receive loving relationship.

He spoke to the woman at the well who had many husbands in a shame-free way that caused her to embrace the Kingdom of God with open arms. By disarming shame, it opened up the door for her to deal with her life, rather than cover it up.

To the woman caught in the very act of adultery, Jesus got

rid of all the shame-based accusers by asking, "He who is without sin, cast the first stone." Getting free from shame recognizes that we all have battles. The moment we act like we don't is the moment the Pharisaical ways of shame are built.

Living without shame must be an intentional process. It takes a decision from each person to move into a new direction. Getting shame off of my life has been one of the most purging experiences of my life. I love equipping people to develop shame-free zones, so that others can work through their issues in safety.

Here are some helpful tips to rid ourselves of shame based thinking.

Become soberly aware that shame has kept us from being real with God and those we need to open up to. Until then, we will continue to play the game of hide and seek with the tender areas of our heart. No progress is truly made until this cloak is removed.

Cultivate a lens of sin separation in how we view ourselves and others. We have to recognize that we may have sin working in our lives, but we are not sin. I may have anger working through me, but I am not anger. You may have lust flowing through your body, but you are not lust. You and I have to see ourselves and the identity we carry in Christ Jesus. Any of the other junk is simply interference, looking to find attachment to us. Recognizing that we may have sin, but we are not sin, disarms shame from accusing us day and night.

Develop a personal revelation of God's love, so we can have the courage to come out of darkness. When we feel safe, we let down our walls and allow ourselves to be vulnerable. Only in God are we completely safe, yet this gets processed out by how we interact with people. Shame tells us to avoid vulnerability with people at all costs. God says, "With me, you are always safe." Beating shame involves receiving the love that God has for you. He never shames and never uses shame to communicate with you.

Get into the light. This is probably the biggest step. We have to move from our hiding places and into a more honest and vulnerable posture. The reason most people's relationships are cruddy is because there is a low level of honesty that has capped the relationship. Two people cannot be truly honest with each another, so the hiding games continue.

I am not advocating that you have to be an open book to everyone you interact with. People need to demonstrate that they are trustworthy. If you become vulnerable and get a shame response, this shows they are not capable of interacting without shame. That person may not be safe at this time. But don't let it stop you from growing in vulnerability.

Utilize the power of confession. You won't find this with the masses, but with a small few. I encourage people to find someone; one or two people who can be light-bearers of healing. Open up and take the risk to be more honest and transparent. Little steps at a time are wise, so that people can demonstrate if they are safe. Breathe in the freedom and celebrate attempts at being vulnerable. Even if you get a less than desirable response, congratulate yourself for taking the brave step.

I remember times where I opened myself up to someone and got a ridiculous response. It's happened to me many times. I drew back in humiliation, blaming myself for ever sharing. But then I stopped beating myself up and actually congratulated my decision to take the risk. Eventually down the road, I was able to land with people that were shame-free and could talk openly about struggles.

Become a shame free vessel for others to become vulnerable. The best way you can do this is to not react in shock to other people's baggage. The moment we treat someone like they have the plague, others will withdraw and wish they never shared. The best way to respond is to listen and love. Don't give the blank stare and don't demean other people's battles. Honor and protect the vulnerable places they reveal to you.

People who come to my wife and I for help are amazed at how we don't shame people. That's because we aren't afraid of sin. We work tenaciously to live shame-free with each other and this carries out towards those that we help.

We are nowhere near perfect, but we have given each other permission to talk about anything and everything with each other. The more we are able to bring issues into the light, the quicker we demolish the problem and move forward.

Be willing to take the first step. It usually takes one brave person to start things off, then others can jump into the invitation to live shame-free. When I first got married, I carried a lot of religious shame, due to some of my church upbringing. I felt shame about everything. I had a lot of condemning thoughts, guilt ridden feelings and shame programming that left me in a hot mess. I carried shame about things I had done and things that I had not done. Shame seemed to cover everything.

This caused me to fear intimacy. So when I got married, I was constantly afraid of my wife, which most men are. I was afraid that if she knew any thoughts or struggles I had, she would reject me and withdraw from connection. This drove me nuts and stole my peace, so I knew I had to act firmly to get free.

I began to take risks and share vulnerable things with Melissa. Her responses were incredibly shame-free and therefore it was easy for me to reciprocate. As I interacted with her in a shame-free manner, she was able to feel safe. The two of us began to share our hearts in a much deeper way. I believe a lot of married couples do not feel close, because they live in fear and shame over things going on in their personal life. They do not want their spouse to know, so they hide. But then they wonder why they struggle with intimacy.

We developed a value in our marriage that we would be willing to talk about anything and process through whatever needs to be addressed. It has taken some very scary risks to solidify this, but every step has been worth it all. To this day, I feel comfortable to share anything that is going on in my heart with Melissa. I feel she is free to do the same. I love her more than ever and I believe that this step has taken our covenant to a new level.

Exercise a new shame-free response. Instead of cowering back, become intentional in practicing vulnerability with others. Create a new reflex. The moment you feel the need to hide, do the reverse and see what kind of amazing freedom it brings. As others share with you, show a shame free response by celebrating vulnerability.

Where are your accusers? Go and sin no more . . .

QUESTIONS FOR CONSIDERATION

1. What has shame done in your life to keep you from being vulnerable?

2. Can you remember a time that you tried to be transparent about a struggle in your life, only to get a response from someone that made you feel worse?

3. In what way can you begin facing some of your own personal shame struggles?

4. How can you create a shame-free environment in your relationships?

5. If shame was broken off all the people that you knew, what can you imagine would become possible?

6. What step can you take today to overcome shame's effects in your life?

PRAYER

Father God, I recognize that shame does not come from You. God, You do not shame us, condemn or guilt us into changing. You love us and pour Your mercy and grace out upon us, so that we may change in a shame-free environment. Thank You for not accusing me and shaming me in my sin. I am grateful that in Your light, there is absolute love and safety. I do not need to be afraid to come to You, fully exposed. Help me to face the fears I have that keep shame intact. Give me a personal revelation of what it means to walk free from shame living and into the light of Your love. I thank You for it, in Jesus name, amen.

05

The Twisted Self

I don't see myself, I see a distorted version of myself.
- Unknown

I know I shouldn't pay attention. But I can't deny what I feel,
even if it isn't real.
- Busted Halo

The most challenging thoughts to discern are the negative ones we have about ourselves. They can become so familiar; we fail to notice the voice has been programming us with a virus of thinking. Toxic thoughts can pulsate through our system so rapidly; connecting to our body and affecting us in ways we don't even realize.

It can be easier to identify certain negative thoughts as coming from the enemy, because they operate clearly as attacks against us. Fear comes upon us. Lust floods our system. Anger rises up inside. These can be easier to label.

A resistance to self-love can be challenging to identify because it doesn't manifest as an offensive attack, but more as a defensive blocker. It deploys a resistance to the presence of love.

The enemy's assignment here is to stand as a hindrance to love, but it can be so subtle. It doesn't make a lot of noise when it operates; because it doesn't need to. The goal is to numb you out from true love.

It takes self-awareness and discernment to recognize this influence. Over time, the resistance to self-love feels like an emotional Plexiglas wall across our chest. For years, I literally felt this physical response. I wanted authentic love, but I could not seem to connect to it from my heart.

Millions live with mindsets that are against themselves and don't know it. Many reject who they are all day long and have no clue this is occurring. The destruction work is quiet but very deadly. Some may hear its voice screaming, but most of the time, these impressions lurk behind the scenes, whispering venomous thoughts that lurk below the surface, yet infect everything.

THE CURTAIN PULLED BACK

Growing up, detecting self-love struggles was not on my radar, especially because loving myself was seen as arrogant. Instead, I bought into self-hate as a spiritual badge of honor by calling it *dying to self*. In reality, I was allowing death and destruction to rule my thoughts every day. I accepted this dark cloud over my self-image as *just the way life was*. I didn't know I was being conditioned to live separated from love.

During my healing process, I perused the dictionary and copied down all the words which began with "self." I highlighted all the negatively defined words . . . self-hate, self-deprecate, self-reject, etc. I began to see an entire list of thought systems that oppose the work of self-love in people's lives.

Illuminated to the deception, I shouted, "This junk has been working in me!" After this revelation sunk in for a few moments, I looked around and exclaimed, "Oh my; this is working in everyone else too."

This startling awakening clarified to me that this resistance was not just who I was. God created me to be loved and to love. I had an enemy training me to see myself in a way that was less than what God saw.

THE BATTLE OF SELF

As I read through the dictionary and scanned these negative "self" words, I began to put labels to many of the thoughts and feelings I carried that were not healthy regarding myself. This is part of what discernment involves, identifying where thoughts come from and knowing what themes they carry. Putting labels to these negative feelings helped me to see the enemy with greater clarity.

This helped me so much, because I was tired of feeling separated from love. When healthy self-love is not in place, a twisted version of self envelops in our thinking. Over time we live accustomed to the absence of love. We don't know there is a problem because we know of nothing better.

Meanwhile, the enemy is assaulting our thoughts, training us to be hard on ourselves and critical about who we are. Thoughts subtly point out our voice, looks and actions; highlighting features in a negative way. People carry an inner tension that is difficult to shake. We are subtly being trained to live as an enemy to ourselves. We can be easily deceived from knowing this is going on. Others may just live in denial, never admitting they carry a low self-image or lack of love.

SELF-TARGETED ATTACKS

Little did I know that God would use a dictionary search to unveil the enemy's schemes in my life. Most of these strongholds were hidden, until I woke up to what was keeping me from true love and freedom. The more I saw these mindsets as being from the enemy, the more I separated those thoughts and feelings as not my own.

Any word that has "self" at the beginning and carries a negative connotation fits under the umbrella of enemy strongholds when we are not filled with healthy love. The following is a list of common "self" strongholds with some examples of how they manifest. I will share some of my own personal examples as well.

Self-Conflict: you struggle in double-mindedness; are hard on yourself; never sure of yourself or decisions

Common Examples: those who always hesitate in decisions and never step forward; those who constantly beat themselves up; struggling with obsessive thoughts over whether or not you are making right decisions or saying the right thing.

Personal Example: I was incredibly double minded, never able to land on a decision. If something did not work out well, I automatically thought it was because of something wrong I did. I was conflicted over who I was and how I fit into the world around me.

84

Self-Accusation: thoughts that cultivate arguments in the mind that criticize and are condemning. It's the thoughts within that yell and accuse you.

Common Examples: having regular arguments play out in the mind, keeping you from peace, thoughts that accuse your struggles, mistakes and weaknesses.

Personal Example: My mind was daily filled with arguments. Back and forth, back and forth, my mind would be flooded with arguments against myself, created great stress and tension.

Self-Condemnation: carries a lot of religious legalism, blaming one's self, struggling to live in the grace of God, very legalistic regarding self, works in partnership with self-accusation.

Common Examples: being very "black and white" about your thoughts and actions without room for grace; punishing self for wrong actions; seeing yourself and/or others through a very harsh judgment and evaluation.

Personal Example: This came into play for me whenever I would make a mistake or sin. I would immediately turn it into a catastrophe that I had to immediately solve with God or else my relationship with Him was at stake. This caused me to become very religiously obsessive. My relationship with God became based on how well I performed and not on love relationship.

Self-Deprecation: thoughts and words that regularly undervalue or devalue who you are and what you have to offer, can involve putting yourself down.

Common Examples: joking in a way that belittles and lowers your worth; saying things about yourself that defeat your potential; deflecting compliments with a negative response.

Personal Example: my language was very self-defeating. I wanted to go one way but my words kept feeding the negative.

Self-Contempt: thoughts that takes away your value, lower your worth and see you as deserving negative outcomes.

Common Examples: having a disgust about poor decisions and choices you have made; being used to negative things occurring in your life; looking down on yourself.

Personal Example: I attached negative outcomes to something wrong with me or that something in me caused all of it.

Self-Sabotage: thinking, acting and living in such a way to prove one's worthlessness; pushing loving relationship away, due to lack of self-love and value for yourself. A self-sabotage can occur in relationships when others love you more than you are willing to love yourself.

Common Examples: speaking words that defeat the good direction you can be headed to; doing things that make people reject you; picking fights with people, who end up rejecting you; avoiding people who love you.

Personal Example: I would take big steps of faith but at the same time, would talk negatively about the difficulties of the decision. It took me some time to realize that I was defeating the steps of faith I took by the negative talk that followed. I had to align my talk with the faith steps I had taken.

Self-Rejection: starts with not feeling loved and accepted by others, leading you to not loving and accepting yourself.

Common Examples: Interpreting the negative in life as being a result of your flaws and you not being good enough; thoughts like "good things don't happen to me because of who I am" or "I get the short end of the stick all the time" are recurring themes.

Personal Example: I would feel that others did not like me. I automatically thought it's because of something wrong about me and/or something wrong I did. I felt that life didn't work for me because of what was wrong with me.

Self-Bitterness: having harsh and/or hostile thoughts and feelings about yourself; being unable to forgive and grant patience to yourself; very hard on yourself overall.

Common Examples: carrying a very tense, stressed and angry presence throughout the day. Being too hard on yourself, which can eventually flow out into relationships.

Personal Example: My whole body would just be tense throughout the day. I was hard on myself, never really giving myself much room for mistakes, imperfection or weakness.

Self-Anger: typically, pent up anger; anger that gets shoved down but will at some point explode.

Common Examples: those who shove down their pain instead of processing it out end up carrying pent up anger, those who struggle with being angry about their life and circumstances; we project so much animosity towards others, when in reality we are actually angry with ourselves; creates physical tension.

Personal Example: Whenever life was difficult or disappointing, I would just let the anger over the pain fume inside me. I didn't want to hurt others, so I would just hold it inside. Little did I know I was damaging myself and eventually others, by not letting these areas get healed in love.

Self-Resentment: keeping a recorded memory of wrongs against yourself; being very aware of your flaws, mistakes and errors with little room for moving past them.

Common Examples: carrying a database of memories that replay mistakes, flaws and weaknesses with a negative emphasis. These memories easily kick up and are hard to shake off.

Personal Example: I had a list of relational mess-ups or embarrassing moments in my past that would torment me in constant replay.

Self-Hate: to love yourself in a lesser way than God intended; not loving or even liking yourself; love being withdrawn towards yourself; reinforces self-bitterness

Common Examples: doesn't allow you to look in the mirror and like what you see, cultivates irritability so that you are not able to love others with kindness and patience, anywhere we struggle to love and accept ourselves, self-hate is present.

Personal Example: I learned over the years that when I was overly tense and irritable, that it was self-hate keeping me in that state.

Self-Retaliation: reacting to circumstances with hostility towards self.

Common Examples: first response after a difficult situation

is to blame self or unleash on self; saying things like, "How could I have been so stupid!"

Personal Example: I would get so upset over simple things. I also had a habit of continually mulling over imperfections of my past that would not allow me to move forward. I can even remember conversations or relational conflicts where I would walk away so tensed up, because I would beat myself up over the issue.

Self-Violence: thoughts and actions that fuel violence against self.

Common Examples: pushing yourself too far, to the point that you damage your body, those who struggle with cutting, self-mutilating or damaging themselves.

Personal Example: Because of my lack of self-love, I would often push myself at work to great extremes; there was a deep part of me that was earning 'penance' through intense activity. Unhappy with my sense of worth, I would pour intensely and "violently" into work, hoping to get validation from those efforts.

Self-Murder: the end goal of self-bitterness, thoughts that reinforce that you should not be alive on this planet, that it would be better if you're life ended.

Common Examples: suicidal struggles, thoughts that say, "others around me would be better off if I was not around;" listening to thoughts that promote death and darkness, not life.

Personal Example: Years ago, I struggled with not wanting to live. I carried a hopeless sorrow in me, no matter what was going on around me. I had so much I could rejoice in, but this self-murderous stronghold kept death and darkness around, never allowing me to breathe in the life available to me.

SELF-DEFEATING TALK

The biggest way we can discern "self-junk" is in our language. How we talk about ourselves, our lives and those around us reveal where "self" monsters are lurking. Too much of our talk today is negative and self-defeating. The good we desire becomes sabotaged by poisonous and negative words we continue to speak.

When I personally coach someone, I teach them to monitor the way they talk to and about themselves. This involves two forms of self-talk; inner and outer self-talk.

Outer self-talk includes the words we say out loud that reflect how we see ourselves. Many have recurring statements they express that carry subtle, yet destructive effects to who they are. In my home, I am teaching my children to watch over how they speak about themselves, for it forms how they will function in life.

I also prescribe that we become more aware of our *inner self-talk*, those unspoken words that fly across the background of our minds throughout the day. These behind the scenes thoughts drive much of our life and for so many, their self-talk is incredibly negative and self-defeating.

Toxic patterns are reinforced in our negative speech. Listen to your daily dialogue and you will hear it—unkind words about yourself that depict a negative tapestry over your life. There is no way to manifest change unless we begin to confront our negative

90

self-talk.

Here are some of the common statements many say that keep life and love from flowing through them.

What's wrong with me?

I can never get this right.

Nothing works out for me.

It doesn't matter.

I can't do this!

I cannot deal with this anymore.

People don't care.

People don't love me.

Others would be better with me not around.

I'm done with this.

As we will see later, one of the keys to experiencing self-love is to speak words over ourselves that are filled with kindness and patience. We cannot allow abusive words about ourselves to continue if we expect to experience the fullness of love in our lives.

A WORLD OF SELF

One of the greatest dangers of people not loving themselves is that eventually society embraces a twisted definition of self-love. Without self-love as God designed it, we become trained to live in a world of "self" focused thinking. This conditions us to have a constant preoccupation with ourselves.

The enemy loves to drive broken people into a world of self-absorption; living in a constant obsession of their inward torment and unease. They become deeply deceived, thinking they are manifesting self-love, when in reality, they are living in downright selfishness. You can see how this twisted assault can leave a person in a lot of confusion.

Healthy self-love does not lead one to be self-consumed. Those who really know how to love themselves are actually very extravagant with how they love others. They know how to live where they prefer others better than themselves in a healthy way. They even know how to lay down their lives in powerful ways.

When people do not engage what love really is, they can fall into a preoccupation with themselves. Their thoughts swirl around with, "what am I feeling," "look at what I am going through" and "how will this affect me" kind of obsessions.

This mindset teaches us to be extremely "me" focused in everything, to the point that love is not allowed to flow through. We become so busy focusing on our pain we have no ability to see the people right in front of us who need relationship.

This is where modern culture lies today. We have become incredibly self-centered, selfish, entitled and narcissistic. In response to humanity's brokenness, we have developed a "me" focus in all relationships. This has formed a self-idolatrous narrative.

What's in it for me?

How does this person make me feel?

What am I getting out of all this?

Am I really happy?

My pain, my feelings, my story . . .

Me . . . Me . . . Me . . . My . . . My . . . My . . . I . . . I . . . I

SELF-FOCUSED BONDAGE

The way people live today, you would think human beings do not even need relationship. We've become so focused on ourselves. Our lives have become isolated, thinking we are safe. This is the goal of the enemy: to block us from love and prevent us from being the powerful, loving vessels we were intended to be.

I read a story from a well-known Christian leader who came to a startling realization regarding his interactions with other ministers and Christian leaders. Over time, he noticed his unaddressed brokenness was hindering his ability to help the people who came to him. He was so hurt from his own wounds in life that when he went out with friends who needed help, he was so focused on his hurt that all he did was talk about himself; never realizing they came to him for help and counsel for their own struggles.

I find that when I sit down and meet with someone for a casual gathering, too often they spend the entire time talking about themselves or their own opinions. They rarely come up for air or take two minutes to ask about me or show concern about my life. I am not talking about people who come to me specifically for help. These are simply casual conversations with fellow brothers and sisters. I could literally go to sleep, wake up and they would still be talking about their life, issues and opinions.

But I understand, because I was there. Years ago, in the depths of my self-love struggles, I became obsessed with myself. I was in such pain and emotional struggle; I spent about 95% of the day thinking about myself. It made me a terrible friend and caused me to miss out on valuable relationships. I was smothered so deeply in my junk that I could not seem to think about what others were going through and how I could help. It was only when I began to focus on loving others, that I got my mind off of self-absorption. It opened the door for the healing process to escalate. I had to see that my deliverance would not happen apart from engaging people in healthy relationship.

THE REMEDY

In response to our brokenness, we often think we need to work on loving ourselves perfectly *before* we can ever love on someone else. This leads to isolation, more than a balanced perspective. I have learned first-hand that in order to experience healing; I have to go beyond myself and love others. I must stop being afraid of how dangerous people are and get back in the game. The key is that when I begin to love on others, I cannot help but allow love have its work in me.

Loving ourselves is directly connected to loving others and being available for others to love us. The key is not just loving others; I had to position myself to allow others to love me. When I did this, a startling revelation occurred to me: bunches of people around me truly loved me! I didn't see it for so long. The lies of the enemy convinced me that I was all alone. The veil came off when I first positioned myself to love others and also allow them to love me.

94

If they didn't love me back, it's ok. I was still loved by God.

SELF-PRESERVATION

Too many are living in self-preservation and protection mode. This is totally counter-cultural to the Kingdom of God. Jesus said in the Gospels that if you try to save your life, you'll lose it[1]. We spend so much time trying to preserve ourselves from being hurt, from feeling pain or being inconvenienced that we actually lose our life in the process. Jesus was teaching that we need to lose our life for His sake, in order to gain life.

But what does that mean?

In practical terms, *losing our life* can teach us to give up the survival tactics we use in relationships. We quit trying to protect ourselves everywhere we go, because our fortresses have become prisons. We are preoccupied with avoiding hurt and thus have wasted our energy. No one can completely avoid being hurt. It's a part of life.

This *losing our life* means letting go of trying to guard all our hurts and prevent ourselves from ever having something negative happen to us. We let go of trying to preserve our image or reputation. We let it go.

One of the qualities that love brings is that we can learn to let go and fall into the arms of God's love for us. We trust that He will walk us through the storms of life so we don't have to preserve our life on our own. If we get hurt, we know we have a Father we can run to for healing.

---

[1] Matthew 16:25

Those who are tempted with a "kingdom of self," have to learn to truly *die to self*, as spoken of in the Scriptures. But we must apply this in the true spirit of what Jesus is helping us to do.

This dying is not self-mutilation or self-rejection. It actually involves dying to those areas that God did not create us with. It speaks of dying to the needs that we keep demanding be fulfilled by others. Oftentimes the areas of woundedness become a vortex of need. Only God can fill those holes, but we have to die to demanding that people be the ones to fill those deep needs.

Part of learning to love ourselves involves balancing the pendulum swings we can fall into. When people recognize they need to love themselves more, they can often make the mistake of isolating in order to heal. They push the pendulum to an opposite place of error. The solution to loving yourself does not involve completely removing yourself from people. In fact, people *are* a part of the remedy!

As we die to the defensive mechanisms and our survival tactics, we let go of avoiding people and we allow ourselves to bless others. When you love yourself, other people's junk no longer becomes a huge threat. We don't waste any more time mulling over how toxic other people are. We begin to think of ways we can truly bless others and make a difference in their life. We give to those who are willing to receive and we don't sweat the ones that won't. We spend less time worrying about the harm people can do to us and more time discovering what love looks like, extended to each person uniquely. It means we focus more on what love can offer, rather than on what dangers "lurk out there", in the world of people.

Becoming others-minded is a great way to break free. Love has its ultimate work when we give out of the overflow of our hearts towards others. Loving yourself does not mean drawing attention to yourself or living in narcissistic ways. It means you are giving out of what you have said *yes* to in your own life. Frederick Collins said, "There are two types of people – those who come into a room and say, *well, here I am*, and those who come in and say, *there you are*." I believe that when you truly settle the self-love issue, you learn how to live with both types operating in your life.

QUESTIONS FOR CONSIDERATION

1. Where do you find the trap of being hard on yourself creeping up the most in your life?

2. What is the biggest self-targeted attack you struggle with and how does it manifest?

3. What examples do you find in yourself and/or in others where we can become very self-focused, coming out of an inability to give and receive healthy love?

4. What is one step you can take today to walk free of a "self" battle you face?

5. In what way can you move from a self-preserving mindset and more into letting love flow through you to others?

PRAYER

Father God, I know that when I am not living in the power of love, my thoughts can be vulnerable to the enemy's ways. I know there is no thought that you have towards me that is not filled with love; because love is who You are. Please expose the battles that keep me locked in myself and unable to walk free in love. Show me where I have allowed self-targeted attacks to keep me locked up in a prison. Show me where I have been self-focused or filled with pride, so that I may humble myself and walk in freedom. Reveal Your heart to me and may I experience love in a deeper way. I choose today to say "no" to all mindsets and ways of thinking that block me from love. I declare war, not on my true self, but on the enemy that war against me. I want to be free today, in Jesus name, amen.

06

Are You Worth Being Loved?

If only you could sense how important you are to the lives of those you meet; how important you can be to people you may never even dream of. There is something of yourself that you leave at every meeting with another person.
— Fred Rogers

You can be the most beautiful person in the world and everybody sees light and rainbows when they look at you, but if you yourself don't know it, all of that doesn't even matter. Every second that you spend on doubting your worth, every moment that you use to criticize yourself; is a second of your life wasted, is a moment of your life thrown away. It's not like you have forever, so don't waste any of your seconds, don't throw even one of your moments away.
— C. JoyBell C.

Growing up, I have had defining moments, where someone spoke powerful words over my identity and my potential. Quite often, it allowed me to see a potential I did not previously see.

Those moments have been critical for my journey. Even to this day, I love speaking over the potential of others and breathing life into what God can do through them.

For so many it has stirred a great awakening. My heart gushes out over the divine promise people carry. Others around them would "amen" these words, as they too can see the greater potential in them. In my pastoral church work, I would gain such joy over what I could see in others. It was so fun to share it and breathe life into their journey.

Using our words to speak over who people really are in God is one of the most powerful experiences. In those moments, we are given an invitation to climb higher out of seeing ourselves differently.

Now this all sounds great, but I got to be honest. I hit a wall.

Over and over again, I noticed a toxic pattern working in the hearts of people. I was dumbfounded to witness what was occurring. A great number of people would not receive the words spoken over them. They literally could not perceive the greater picture. Not even a glimpse. It was almost like they turned their senses off and shut down when others would see greatness in them. To make matters worse, many were not even interested in learning to see it.

That was the hard part. Not only were they incapable of seeing it. They showed no desire to explore any more than what they were living in.

I began to ask God about this.

What in the world is going on here? If people don't see what You see in them, they will remain stuck and stagnant their whole life!

As I continued to search out this issue, I began to see the battles over their lives. It was like spiritual 3D glasses were put on my eyes. The enemy had developed a stronghold of unworthiness that would cause them to deflect any love, goodness or divine potential God would send their way. Their brokenness conditioned them to know nothing better for themselves.

My heart sunk as I witnessed this. I spent months and years crying out to God about this block; mourning the hearts of people that sat in church services like drones. I looked at teachers, pastors, business owners, prophets and apostles in the making, right in front of me. I saw it. But they couldn't see it. What pierced my heart was knowing they were not really interested in seeing it. All they saw was the lower identity they lived from. Nothing more.

WE'RE NOT WORTHY

The resistance they carried had trained them to never receive the fullness of what Christ paid for, leaving them to manifest a lower-level identity. With it came less potential and little impact. It taught them to be ok with not progressing. They took the life of a slave rather than a son.

How could someone throw away this divine invitation to greatness?

When people are used to simply getting by, never entering into the fuller dimension of love, they become used to dwelling in a lower level of living. The more you get used to this, the less you are open to any hope of something greater.

A lot of people live in this, thinking they are being humble, but it's a false humility. They think they are being good servants. When in reality, they are giving up their divine birthright.

Unworthiness will not allow them to engage the divine identity and destiny over their lives. They instead give into a lesser view of themselves, with little hope, no risk and small faith.

We live our lives out of how we see ourselves and how we think God sees us. Unworthiness blocks us from seeing God's perspective of us and keeps us in a pauper's mindset, never stepping up to the high place that God has prepared for us.

We remain in thoughts like, "I'm just a sinner" or "it's not me it's the Lord." We can add in my favorite distorted Scripture, "He must increase. I must decrease." Unworthiness trains people to stand in the back, so they are never set up for blessing and breakthrough.

Unworthiness says, "If it's God's will, it will just happen."

Faith says, "God said you are worthy because of His Son. Now take hold of everything He says you have. Position yourself in all things for His goodness to flow to you and through you." Unworthiness doesn't hear the words of faith, because it has conditioned a person to live in unbelief over their potential. The worst part is they live thinking it's acceptable to not even search it out.

Most people with unworthiness in their lives very often do not see the power they have in who they are. They see very little influence in their voice, so they don't bother talking. They see no difference their presence makes, so they show up late, or don't bother showing up at all. They accept lesser living because their lesser identity tells them their actions, good or bad, don't make a difference.

They don't realize they have a voice. Because of this, they rarely speak up or use their mouth to stir up others into change. This keeps people bound in a world of spiritual slavery that knows nothing better.

People who have unworthiness are quick to disqualify themselves. They see their tattered past as a liability to the Kingdom of God, forgetting that everyone God used in the Bible had issues. Unworthy-minded people see weakness as a bad thing, rather than a place God can work the most. They have a hard time accepting themselves. On top of it all, they don't really face these struggles and work to overcome them.

The unworthy mindset teaches us to take the road of least resistance. They end up living their life passively, never pressing into breakthrough or fighting for what God says is available. When the call is made to stand up for what is better, they will only engage it if it's easy.

That's one of the problems of breaking free. If I have to get rid of unworthiness, that means I am responsible to step forward and activate who I am in God. I have to face my fears, insecurities and hang-ups, while also being willing to take risks, make mistakes and at times be vulnerable in my weaknesses. Unworthiness scares people into a passive false comfort, which requires no responsibility.

THE PASSIVITY OF UNWORTHINESS

I ran into this issue head on during a painful teaching experience years ago. I remember a particular church service, where I called out the divine potential of the men in the meeting. The intent of my summons was to draw men out of their passivity and see their call of leadership in the Kingdom.

The more I talked, the more resistance rose in the room. I could feel the unworthiness and passivity as thick as ice in the room. Regardless, I passionately declared a greater picture of who God saw them to be and the call He had over their identity. The more I spoke, the more I saw their discomfort, because my message meant getting out of passivity and into obedience to the higher calling.

When I speak in front of crowds, I often have the audience engage the message with some kind of response, to activate the truth that God is saying. In this situation, I made a plea for men to stand in agreement with me, as I lifted one arm straight up in the air and held it high. My call was for men to see the identity that God had placed on their lives and make a stand as leaders.

The fire of God was so hot on me, I thought, "Not only is every man going to stand up. Every woman will probably stand too." That's how much faith was in me.

I stood there a little longer than usual, waiting for the men to rise. I continued to stand, for what seemed like forever, hoping that at least a couple guys would get up. As time passed, I stood with my hand in their air, which was getting tired at this point. I'm thinking, "I made this call as clear as I can make it. What is going on here?"

Seconds turned into minutes and minutes into an eternity. *Can at least one guy give me a courtesy stand...just so this doesn't become a complete embarrassment?* I began to weep internally as not one man stood to his feet. Part of me wanted to just leave the room, because it was so painful. I don't know why, but I continued to stand there. Maybe it's my stubborn Puerto Rican/Norwegian genetics, I am not sure. But I do know it was one of the most sobering and heart-grieving experiences of my life. Unworthiness had made the men so passive. They were spiritually taken out.

I grieved the war that was taking place over them. The women in the room began to cry out to God over the hearts of the men. They didn't condemn them nor accuse them in guilt. One by one, they simply prayed out loud for their hearts to be open to love and the identity that God gave them. I wasn't sure whether to cry or scream.

The service ended with not a single male responding. I witnessed first-hand the absolute battle waging over this issue. At first, I beat myself up over this problem, thinking if I had just done something different, things would be better. Over time, God had to heal my heart from that experience. I learned painfully that day, you cannot want something for someone more than they do, no matter how much you love on them.

At the end of the day, we all have a responsibility to receive the love that God has for us and connect to what love leads us into. In that love, our truest identity is forged. When we grasp who we are in the love of God, we are now responsible to step forward in accordance with that new identity. We cannot tolerate the old identity any longer.

Because so many have not been rooted in love, they live in alignment with their counterfeit identity. That old identity is what they've always known, so they remain comfortable in it, even though it's slowly killing them. Unworthiness keeps us locked into those old ways, training us in a passive lifestyle, involving little risk, adventure or courage. Billions live in this slavery position. Nothing gets stretched in their life. They run from challenges. They take the road of least resistance; therefore, so little change occurs. The narrative of their life is, *sittin' on your biscuit, never havin' to risk it.*

DON'T BE DECEIVED

When you see unworthiness on someone, a typical response is to be moved with compassion. Initially, this is good, because love is the answer. But you have to remember that unworthiness paints a "poor me" picture to draw the sympathy and compassion out of people. Of course we need to continually have compassion for those who struggle in this area, but don't be fooled, this stronghold has no intention of leaving. This unworthiness is a sinister demonic force that works to keep people blocked from love and the identity God has given them.

Looking from the outside, your first response is to extend the love of God and help paint a picture of the person's higher identity. But be forewarned; unworthiness is extremely stubborn and will keep itself intact. You can actually drain yourself emotionally trying to convince them unless the person takes full responsibility to move into understanding and activating their God-given identity.

If they do not take responsibility, they will become defensive about their brokenness. If someone touches on the unworthy areas of their heart, pride kicks up to protect the wound. The person switches from being a helpless casualty to a flawless saint. The victim mindset is still there, it's just hiding.

Pride does everything it can to block and keep people from seeing that a person really doesn't love who they are. If people around are not discerning, this pattern will deceive everyone. This is the problem; unworthiness carries a hidden world of stubborn pride.

That's why the only way to get free in the area of self-love is to humble ourselves in the deepest place of our heart. We must humble ourselves before God and let that be reflected in our relationships with others.

Both God and people are needed in the transformation process. Healthy people are needed in our lives to free us. Some of you reading this may need to see a greater value for relationships. You isolate yourself in self-protection so that no one has the ability to love you.

Humbling myself means I see value in relationships in a whole new way. It doesn't mean I now draw on people like a suction valve. It means I give a vulnerable self to people so that I can face my fears and most of all, face the toxic ways of my heart so I can change. Breaking self-love struggles cannot be done in isolation. Relational interaction is the incubator for spiritual change.

As I humble myself in relationships, I become teachable in how to move towards healthy self-love. This involves shifting my relational style. I cannot move away from compliments, intimacy or vulnerability. Where I once ran, I must interrupt that dysfunctional pattern and work through my insecurities. Everything in my life must be willing to change. If we keep protecting everything, we allow those dysfunctional areas to fester and grow as a dominating force. But when I change my perspective of relationships to be a place for my healing, I no longer see people as enemies but as vessels for my growth.

UNABLE TO RECEIVE

Many are deceived, because in certain moments, they feel they can love on others, leading them to believe they possess love for themselves. It's important to know that loving on someone in a moment of prayer or ministry help does not mean we know how to love ourselves. It can be easy to stir up love for someone in a brief moment, yet much deeper to carry a continual reservoir of love for people on a daily basis in our lives. This is where the battle wages.

Scores of believers all over the world give of themselves in loving ways to people, while at the same time struggling to possess love for themselves. We mistake the gifts of the Holy Spirit operating through us as proof that we love ourselves with God's love.

The gifts of God by their very nature display the love of God for two main reasons. First, they minister blessing to people no matter where they are at in their journey. Second, the gifts of God operate effectively whether the one ministering is in a good place or not. That's why the Bible says the *gifts of God are without repentance* (Romans 11:29). In other words, your life can be an absolute mess and the gifts of God will still operate through you. Why? This is the power of grace, where He works through you in your imperfect state, as you learn to grow.

But we can be deceived. We can think that because gifts work through us, we carry the love of God for ourselves in our hearts. I have personally helped hundreds of people who are able to minister in such power, yet struggle to have a heart full of love for themselves. They pour out to others but are disconnected in having that in their own lives.

This heart neglect is what we need to see. You can touch hundreds and thousands of people with the gifts of God and still neglect the work of love for yourself in your own heart. I am reminded of 1 Corinthians 13, where Paul reminds us that love is always the more excellent way.

Though I speak with the tongues of men and of angels, but have not love, I have become sounding brass or a clanging cymbal. And though I have the gift of prophecy, and understand all mysteries and all knowledge, and though I have all faith, so that I could remove mountains, but have not love, I am nothing. And though I bestow all my goods to feed the poor, and though I give my body to be burned, but have not love, it profits me nothing.[1]

Wait! Give your body to be burned? I can understand the other examples, but, offering your body to be sacrificed? Wouldn't that be the ultimate act of love? Didn't Jesus die as an ultimate act to display the love of God through Him?

Yes, it is possible to give yourself out passionately, even to the point of becoming a martyr, yet not possess the power of love. I believe a couple reasons influence this.

---

[1] 1 Corinthians 13:1-3 NKJV

1. Too many people strive to do something to *earn* love. They have not learned to receive love, so they think by their acts of heroism, they will arrive in a place of being loved and accepted. This is the performance lifestyle, where we don't know how to be loved, so we do something for love in most areas of our life. We think the solution to our love void is to do something to make ourselves worthy of being loved.

2. It is possible to do incredible acts of love, yet not possess love from God for ourselves. We can easily minister to people and help others so much that we neglect the life of our own heart. Ask most believers, "How is your heart doing?" and you will usually hear performance answers (what they are doing) or condemning answers (the yucky areas they are continually ashamed about).

No one has taught us to stop and address our lack of self-love. Mentors, fathers and mothers have not fully nurtured us into what a life of being loved looks like; therefore, we end up becoming clanging cymbals—making a lot of noise, but not embedding the work of love into our hearts.

If I pour love out to others and do not love myself, I am living in a misplaced flow. I cannot give to others what I have not processed through in my own heart. Otherwise I live in plastic Christianity and will eventually fall into burnout and disillusionment.

I remember most of my life, when someone would complement or say kind words to me, I would often deflect it right back to them or defer to a flaw. *Well, I could have done it better. . .* I ignorantly thought I was being humble until I realized, *I don't know how to let someone love me.*

God will still work through you if you love others but not yourself. That's how amazing He is. But we lose the value of having a fuller life and immersing ourselves in the "more excellent way" that Paul spoke of in the book of 1 Corinthians[1].

Do not be lured into thinking that because people are being touched by your life, that you know how to love yourself. The fruit of true self-love shows in how you are able to accept yourself, how you are able to receive love from others and how you get your value from simply being loved.

Every time you help someone, it should be a reminder to engage God's love for yourself. We can no longer expect people to position themselves to be loved while we ignore that need in our own hearts. We cannot call ignoring our own heart a noble cause.

Go love and be loved needs to be the new theme.

The reality is, love is looking for you, but are you ready to receive it? Have you positioned yourself to say yes to love?

If so, you are saying yes to God and yes to what He says. We cannot tell others to receive from God what we ourselves are not opening our hearts to take in.

Are you willing to posture your heart to say yes to love?

WHERE DO YOU GET YOUR SELF-WORTH?

I don't know about you, but over the years, I have wrapped my self-worth in so many different things that never satisfied.

---

[1] 1 Corinthians 12:31-13:13

111

We always seem to get trapped in counterfeit sources of worth. We look to our job, friendships, level of success (whatever that means) and status symbols to feed the empty space. But it's like giving pure white sugar to a hungry child. They get a burst, but gain no nutrition or lasting satisfaction.

When we are not loved in who we are, we lack the understanding of where to find value. Our compass for daily satisfaction and happiness is guided by counterfeit sources of worth. Because of this, our sense of true-north is off, leading us to winding trails that lead nowhere. That's why we can put so much effort into life yet still not feel fulfilled. Our worth is rooted in the wrong place.

We have to understand that our mode of finding self-worth can come from God, but it can also come from counterfeit sources. When the counterfeit gets our attention, we look for our worth in the evaluations of others. We throw ourselves into performing and pleasing people. Status means more than it should. We live in a world of achievement to cover our lack of self-worth. Positions and titles become appealing. Hearing people validate us no longer becomes an added bonus in life. It becomes our emotional oxygen.

When we get hits of the counterfeit, we feel a temporary rush that seems to alleviate the inner need. Yet these areas never satisfy in the long run and they often become idols; usually taking our eyes off of God and on to what we don't have in life. In the end, we feel separated from God's love and the love of others.

To move into victory, we must intentionally receive the love that God has for us, by saying "yes" in our hearts to that love. We also need to position ourselves in relationship to be loved and to love without fear or discomfort getting in the way. We cannot allow the enemy to keep us in a lesser identity of unworthiness. We must declare that our Father in heaven deems us worthy, especially because of what His Son provided for us.

QUESTIONS FOR CONSIDERATION

1. Where do you find yourself resisting the greater picture over your life? Where do you see others doing this?

2. In what ways do we often live out of a lesser identity in our life? Why do people tend to fall into this regularly?

3. Where do you find people can easily try to love on others while ignoring themselves?

4. In what ways do you find yourself coming into agreement with unworthiness?

PRAYER

Father, I recognize that unworthiness is not of you, where I come into agreement with living in a lesser identity. God, I take responsibility for change today. I recognize that resisting Your love and calling it humility is wrong. I no longer want to fight the love and identity that You have for me. I repent of and renounce any agreement with unworthiness, in my life and stemming from previous generations. This pattern of unworthiness stops with me. I ask God that you cleanse my life from thinking and behavior that is based on unworthiness. Let the power of Your love flow mightily through me, that I may be a vessel of love to all I see. I command all works of unworthiness to leave now. I am loved and will be loved!

07

The Hidden Villain

To not love is to hate.
- unknown

Self-hatred is a tragedy.
- Elizabeth Hardwick

No one could hate me as much as I hate myself.
- unknown

Hate?! That's a strong word! I don't hate myself!

This is the response I get from many who discover the lack of love they have for themselves. It takes some time to realize, when love is not in the mix, hatred seeks to fill that place.

If I were to highlight the most hidden, yet deadly work against self-love, it is the stronghold of self-hatred. It drives so much of how people live today, yet it lives undetected for the most part. Sometimes the enemy's most effective tactic is keeping people from even realizing he is there.

Self-hatred is the biggest reason why people do not love themselves to the fullest. It's like the neighborhood stalker, waiting for any moment when love is not home, so he can run in and inflict bondage. Self-hate creates some of the deepest programming in the mind and actions of those who have not been loved properly.

Once it's exposed, we have a chance to put this thing on the run. That is why I spend so much effort exposing these mindsets. Once you truly identify self-hate as not being you, you have now gained leverage over its attacks. I've helped many pry it out of their heart and minds, but it took some teaching and intentional work to walk free.

I thoroughly enjoy helping people recognize and walk out of this monster's clutches, especially because of what it inflicted in my life for years. Each person who gets free is another act of justice for what the enemy stole in my life. I can literally say I am not the same person and the journey of renewal has been amazing.

In fact, I have felt the greatest amount of change in my emotional state when I cast self-hate away from my thoughts. Sometimes I get so knotted up in its ways I don't realize it snuck in. It's not until I say, "Wait a second! What's going on here?" that I get sobered up to why I am feeling irritable, unlovable or angry.

I see the greatest fruit in my marriage. Melissa and I have witnessed the removal of self-hate as being a major force for strengthening our relationship. When we entertain its dysfunction, we end up in a spiritual Ping-Pong with each other. Our words and actions become dry, cold, defensive and stressed. Strife can fill the air.

Freedom from its deception has allowed us to move into a

greater bond of love. We love each other deeply, but self-hate wants to keep us from being able to walk in dynamic intimacy with each other. We have seen first-hand how the quality of relationship improves when self-hate is removed.

LOST LOVE FOR YOURSELF

To understand self-hate, we need an awareness of the word *hate* that is used in the New Testament Scriptures. In the Greek language of the New Testament, the word *hate* that Jesus often used in passages like Matthew 24, saying many "will hate one another" is the word *Miseō*. This is number g3404 in the Strong's Concordance and is used 41 times in the New Testament. Miseō means to *hate, pursue with hatred or to detest*.

But there is a critical insight to know: **this word for hate also means *to love less*.** Hate involves love growing cold. We are getting a picture here of love being blocked or withdrawn. The Bible says that following this work of people hating more, the love of many will grow cold. Hate's main focus is the removal or withdrawal of love in a relationship dynamic.

So take this word and see what it does in regard to "self." *Self-hate is when you love yourself less.* Whenever you feel emotionally cold or numb about yourself, self-hate is present. When you feel blocked from being able to love and accept yourself, that is self-hate. When love is being withdrawn from how you think about yourself or see yourself, self-hate is the villain feeding your thoughts.

One of the most common deceptions when addressing self-hate is that people say, "I don't hate myself. I just don't really like myself." That is classic self-hate in hiding. If you do not fully love yourself and get excited about who God made you to be, then self-hate has had an influence.

12 COMMON SIGNS OF SELF-HATRED

You don't have to have all these characteristics, but the following patterns will help identify self-hatred mindsets in your life. Our goal is to expose its work and remove it. The following are 12 common manifestations that self-hate is working to keep you from the ability to love yourself.

1. A regular inability to have fun and enjoy life. Joy is a real challenge to manifest. Excitement is not a daily emotion in your life. A lack of personal happiness and pleasantness is very hard to maintain.

2. Difficulty being comfortable when looking in the mirror or seeing a picture of yourself.

3. Struggles with a very negative outlook on life and relationships.

4. Chronic irritability and moodiness.

5. Others feel an underlying anger coming from you. Loved ones and close family usually feel it the most.

6. Constant, overwhelming battles with discouragement, depression or despair.

7. Can do for others but you don't do for yourself. You deflect receiving credit, love and appreciation given from others. Some overcompensate for their self-hate by always giving out, but ignoring their own needs and personal value.

8. Being celebrated and loved on by others makes you feel uncomfortable. You are not always easy to love on. Not because of your flaws, but because of your inability to receive love for yourself.

9. Affection is challenging for you to receive. Having someone hug you or look in to your eyes is very uncomfortable.

10. There are deep patterns of being driven and motivated by perfectionism, performance and/or people pleasing.

11. There is an overall inability to connect from the heart in relationships. Coldness and numbness can be a common emotional issue. In many, there can be a theme of struggling to move towards hope, especially when talking about one's self.

12. You are prone to addictive habits, stemming from your inability to love yourself.

UNCOMFORTABLE WITH LOVE

Self-hate begins with not being loved properly. Millions of people live without realizing what they were missing in their hearts. Then when love presents itself, we become awkward in receiving it.

Having no reference for receiving love, we don't know how to develop intimate relationships. However, even if someone did grow up in a loving home, they may still be vulnerable to self-hate.

Self-hate doesn't care. It will infiltrate any heart where it can find agreement. Out of this dilemma, most people fall into one or more of these three patterns:

1. Self-hate conditions us to be relationally passive. The problem is we don't have a reference for love, so we don't bother. Men notoriously struggle with this and develop a reputation for being unemotional and passive. Society has even become used to men not being able to connect to their hearts and express themselves relationally.

On the other hand, self-hate releases a deluge of bondage over the life of females as well. It works slowly to shut down a woman's heart. Over time, a female gets exhausted from all the disappointments and burdens that weigh on her. Eventually, she will implode unless healing is opened up over her life.

So instead of stepping out into love, we take the passive approach. We avoid intimate moments. We make a joke when someone wants to have heart to heart conversation. We walk out of the room when family or friends want to open up with each other. I've done it. You've done it. We all have.

When someone else is going through pain, we don't know what to say. We either say nothing at all or we give some cliché statement that has no meaning. All because we are actually uncomfortable with love and the vulnerability that love allows.

The Bible says that *a man who loves his wife loves himself.* We can also infer here that a man who does not love his wife in action does *not* love himself. He struggles with self-hatred. In marriage, when a spouse is difficult to deal with or spews out irritable anger, there is usually a self-hatred component involved. It does not want to be exposed, so it spends its energy making the other person the target.

A man who acts unloving towards his wife or does not fight

for her heart, it's usually because he does not love himself. It's why many men destroy their marriage, then stand in sadness, not realizing how their covenant eroded.

This is what fuels the back and forth of strife in marriages. It all starts with two people, coming together, who do not love themselves. They need the other person to love them perfectly, or else they become disgruntled and resentful. Self-hate loves to hide itself by blaming others, usually the ones closest to us.

2. Self-hate trains us to perform. Loving yourself works best when we cultivate self-acceptance unconditionally, without having to earn it. To overcompensate for not liking ourselves, we can easily become submerged into performing. We delve into achievement or work accomplishments. These arenas give us a false and shallow form of affirmation, but they never fill the empty void inside. Many still chase this carrot anyway, because they get a momentary emotional fix from it.

Let's be honest, it's so much easier to go to work and do the motions rather than dealing with emotional issues. Heart connected relationship takes vulnerability and investment. This is why most relationships become stagnant and marriages turn into roommate arrangements.

Unfortunately, we too often attempt to perform for God. When problems arise, we look for some kind of performance-based mechanism to solve the issues. The problem is the whole matrix for living is on the wrong setting. You cannot perform for God, but when you have self-hate, you feel separated from God's love all the time. Therefore, you plunge into doing stuff to alleviate or escape those feelings of separation.

This leads us into the modern day obsession with success. We long to be and look successful. Yet success in God's eyes rarely appears the way we think it should. And it certainly does not come from a heart that is constantly trying to find love and fulfillment through performance.

Self-hate will drive people to live for achievement, as a source of validation and worth. When we lack self-love, we lack identity. When we lack identity, we look for something we do to fill the void.

3. Self-hate fuels our addictive patterns. Instead of turning towards God to fulfill our need to be loved, self-hate leads us into some kind of addiction instead. Behind self-hatred is a lot of inward pain. Instead of facing the pain and dealing with it, the enemy drives us into some kind of pleasure escape. We end up turning to counterfeits instead of true love. Unless we address our broken heart, we will search for pleasure to escape our pain every time.

Notice that people who struggle with addictions have an inability to dwell in stable love? Loving them is like trying to hold on to an eel. They keeping squirming out of your connection. The moment you attempt to get closer, they find a way to avoid it. Maybe you do this with people who attempt to love you.

Living numb or separated from love is an excruciating world to dwell in, so counterfeit coping options can become easy temptations. Sex, work, food, drugs, novels, Netflix . . . anything can become an addiction. The question is, "what are looking to as a way to cope with pain?"

Our generation has become an addict-filled people, because we are unable to process the comfort of self-love. Our lives are filled with so much emotional hurt and very little references for healing. No wonder self-hate easily slips into the picture.

I have helped many people work through addictions by facing the self-hate they carry. Doing this allows their heart to become more open to love, thereby leaving less room for addictions to tempt.

Addictions run in my family and so does self-hate, so I've had to do business with these areas. I spent my younger years struggling with food addictions, obsessive thoughts and sexual temptations like pornography. I ran into a life of performance based living, seeking to earn the love of God and others. This was to overcompensate for my self-hatred. I didn't love myself, so I had to burn the candle relentlessly to feel loved, yet I was never able to feel that love. This drove me into feelings of constant emptiness, burnout and loneliness. Love was not a reference for me, so I had no ability to comfort myself. What I longed for was, loving intimacy, but the enemy drove the counterfeit into my life.

Self-hate trains us to look for something else besides true love for comfort. It never allows you to face yourself with love and get out of your prisons. The enemy wants to keep you trapped. It has only been since I faced those issues that the chains fell off. I was able to move from being tempted on a daily basis, to living a life where that stuff doesn't have a place to land anymore. Why? Because I walked into letting God fill me with a love where I could love and accept myself each day. Love is the answer and until we learn to love ourselves, we don't stand a chance against addictions.

YOUR LIFE DEPENDS ON THIS

Getting free from self-hate is as important as life itself. When you don't like or love yourself, it gives room for hate to roam and it doesn't come alone. Hate, by its very nature, comes to release death upon our lives. 1 John reminds us of the work that hate brings.

*Whoever hates his brother is a murderer...*1 John 3:15

When hate is present, so is murder. With self-hate in the game, self-murder comes right along. This may sound strong to you, but I need to say it straight so we sober up and overcome.

Self-hate opens you up to death. This is because self-hatred is a form of self-death. Removing love is like removing oxygen. We cannot live without it. Self-hate slowly erodes our wholeness, keeping us from a full and healthy life of love. It also carries a hoard of self-loathing, where we look at ourselves, our flaws and errors, with disgust.

Instead of self-compassion, self-loathing points a person towards victim thinking and self-pity as comfort. Instead of picking ourselves up in the love and comfort of the Holy Spirit, self-loathing pushes us down so that we never get up in confidence.

This is where people tragically get stuck. Their inner brokenness is manifesting, but instead of loving themselves into freedom, they loathe their lives throughout the day, wondering why they do not witness change. They also give into a posture of self-pity, hoping someone will rescue them out of their condition, not realizing they have the power to step out themselves.

Self-hate leads people into emotional comas. Their minds can be strong, yet their hearts are far from connecting to the depth of love. So many talk about knowing what love is in their minds, but they have no connection to it in their hearts. Self-hate loves to keep people in this bind. We end up living from a place of theory only, with little actual experience. In fact, the theology of most people is simply theory. They have not had a personal activation in their hearts to encounter the power of the love that is available for them.

LOVING YOURSELF INTO CHANGE

Here is a missing piece to breakthrough. We cannot powerfully change unless we love ourselves into that change. Permanent, long lasting transformation occurs best when love is in the atmosphere. Otherwise we will end up going from one roller coaster to the next, never landing into steady progress.

One of the most powerful lessons I have learned regarding self-love is that change without loving myself wastes my energy and investment. I must love myself into change. Love cultivates the power to change. This takes two experiences.

First, it is critical to love and accept yourself in your current state. No "ifs" or "buts." If you keep hating on yourself for certain flaws, failures or sins, you will actually remain in that bondage. Love needs to be accepted from God for you.

God accepts you in your current condition. Why shouldn't we then receive what our Creator says? Who are we to overthrow what God says about us, when He knows way more about ourselves than we do? Yet He still loves us!

God loves us in our current state to draw us closer into relationship. The enemy will tell you that you need to be more "lovable" in order for that to take place.

God will love you, even if you never decide to love Him back.

God will love you even if you never change.

To push this even further, God will love you, even if you decide to never serve Him!

This may shake people's religious mindsets, but we must understand, God's love for us goes way beyond what we often see exchanged in the lives of individuals.

So I must first accept myself in my current state. The more unconditional the acceptance is; the more powerful self-love is experienced. I cannot keep saying, "I will love myself once I am…" because you will place conditions on love. For too many, they will only accept themselves if certain conditions are met. But they are never met. Even if they are, self-love never arrives. This is the programming of self-hate that has to be erased.

Second, loving yourself will be activated by the powerful decisions you make. The power of love needs to be activated as we make decisions based on healthy love for ourselves.

What does it mean to love myself in my decisions, choices and actions from now on? What behaviors have been rooted in self-hate, where I now need to love myself into change? What am I tolerating because I am not loving myself? This is where we have the opportunity to become empowered to take our life back. We love ourselves enough to take action.

Most people try to change out of self-hate and guilt. They hate how they look so they diet, only to end up back to where they were before, if not worse. Someone hates the way their life is going, and no matter how hard they try, they give into the same patterns that feed the defeated circumstances. If there are any decisions, they are momentary bursts that never last.

Why does this pattern continue for so many?

Until we remove our self-hate conditioning, we will remain stuck. Self-hate constantly accuses, and will never love you into change. It yells at you with no belief you can change and improve.

Accusation never changes us. When was the last time someone accused you and it changed your life for the good? The answer is probably never. Stop listening to hateful thoughts over yourself and tolerating the accusations regarding your shortcoming, sins and weaknesses. It's time to love that hate right out of you.

God leads us from glory to glory as we come into agreement with His love for us. Saying yes to His love allows relationship to form deeply. God cannot and will not transform us apart from relationship. It is in the context of loving relationship that all permanent change takes place.

Every major stage of transformation in my life has come from a place of loving myself. For example, I struggled with food and weight issues all my life. It wasn't until I loved and accepted myself in my struggle, that I then made loving decisions for permanent transformation. After years of trying everything, I started dealing with self-hate issues. Then one day it dawned on me. *Whenever I ate foods that were not the best for me, or ate foods to medicate something in my heart, I was actually hating on myself. I cannot love myself with junk food. If I gave a dog rat food, I would be hating on the dog. If I put peanut butter in my car engine, that would be hating on my car. I don't eat the best because I do not love myself enough to change.*

I struggled for years in trying to live as a morning person, even though I wanted to badly. Like many, I would punch the alarm clock every day and groan getting up. I wanted to get a jump on the day by waking up fresh and early, but I just couldn't seem to break the cycle. I would drag out of bed at the last minute and rush into the day. I would be groggy until midmorning. The lethargy coming from my poor sleeping patterns worked against me every day.

Until one day it dawned on me. *By going to bed late and then not waking up at a good time, I am hating on myself and sabotaging my desire to take on the day. This has to change!*

I loved myself into creating new habits. I decided that getting to bed at a good time was an act of love towards myself. I began to go to bed earlier and wake up at times that were more effective for my daily schedule. I tried for decades to change this, without success. Loving myself into change was the answer!

MAKE THE DECISION

Driving our self-hate is more firmly sealed when we make decisions based on self-love. We have to ask ourselves in every thought, belief and action, "Is this something I would do if I really loved myself? Is this something I would allow if I truly carried self-love?"

This area has hit me personally many times in my life and one big season in my personal history.

In 2006, I left a staff pastoring position and stepped out to start a whole new ministry from scratch. I found myself during those years teaching a weekly conference to a local gathering that carried on for months. During that season, we felt a strong leading to plant a church, out of those who were attending and looking for a home fellowship.

I hesitated to start a church, because it was not my number one calling, but I knew it was needed. I also thought I could possibly raise up people to carry on the church work as I continued to spread teachings of transformation.

If I had a nickel for everyone who said they would jump, back me up and support me, I would be a millionaire. I learned quickly how cheap that talk has become in people. They can easily say something and not follow up on it. Somehow that is deemed acceptable. When it actually came to stepping up and starting this, I noticed many disappeared, got offended or started trouble.

Yet for years, I continued to pour into the people who remained planted and raised up leaders who could carry the work of ministry. It was extremely difficult. Like many pastors, I wanted transformation for the people more than they wanted it for themselves. This was a quick lesson I was learning on the fly.

I also experienced a ton of betrayal, misunderstanding and twisted communication. Most of all, I was hit square in the face with the reality that many people cannot see the big picture that God sees. I walked in with tremendous faith, but over time began to shake my head as to why things seemed to move sluggishly. Over the years, I have learned the hard way that many people want breakthrough, but they want to remain in status quo as far as their own personal change.

I don't hate them for it. Many just didn't have references for going to the next level. Others would need 24/7 help to get to the next level of growth. I was overwhelmed with the lack of spiritual fathering people had and I couldn't be a father to everyone.

In that journey, I got sick a bunch of times. My skin started flaring up and I developed patches all over my body. My joints inflamed and fatigue slammed me. My body struggled with energy and I was worn out almost every day. Not only that, at the time we were coming to an awareness that our first born son Maximus was being diagnosed with autism. My daughter Abigail was born during this time as well. Many new experiences were occurring at the same time. In addition, we were battling our financial state from week to week, wondering how we would be able to break through. I was living in perpetual burn-out.

It seemed like many friends had vanished. Some wouldn't even return correspondence after many calls and emails. Not everyone disappeared, but most did. Just when I needed the greatest amount of help, I felt abandoned. The pain was excruciating.

Meanwhile the church wasn't growing and I was struggling to raise people up to the next level. Week after week, I would walk away shaking my head. God would release what seemed like nuclear power, yet very little change would take place during the week. I studied church growth, fasted and sought after counsel. I left more confused than empowered in most of my interactions.

The self-hate I was freed from before had now come back with a vengeance like a flood. I felt so out of control of the results in my life that I felt trapped. The self-hate moved easily into self-loathing, because I had no idea what to do. Each week, I would attempt a refreshed strategy, only to find myself in the same set of circumstances. An accusing cloud of depression loomed over me day after day, blaming me for everything that was wrong with the church, accusing me in my thoughts for every complaint and every disgruntled person.

I am the kind of person that thinks, "How can I grow through a given situation" rather than pointing fingers. This can work great in most circumstances, but it turned against me. I gave into the mindset that something was wrong with me and things were not moving forward because of all that is flawed in me.

It was during this time that God taught me how to love myself at a deeper level than I ever experienced. He taught me the value of being kind and patient in my inner self-talk. Every time I asked Him for direction, God would respond with how to love myself. Self-hate had snuck back in so it took some time to get it out. Over and over again, I had to stop blaming myself and learn to give myself unconditional acceptance.

This led me to a decision, based on loving myself to an entirely new level. I was led to a courageous step of faith to end our season of pastoring and close the church that we were shepherding. It was one of the toughest decisions to make, but also one of the clearest ones I have made. What gave me the courage to do it was that I came to a place of loving myself as God's child; therefore, I made a decision out of that personal conviction.

What I believe God's purpose was for that church season is probably best left for a future writing. But the key here is that I really had to love myself and kick out self-hate with fury. I had to make a decision for my family and myself. I had to love who

God made me to be and not who people were trying to form me to be for them.

That decision broke the internal conflict off me, and freed me to further pursue what God designed me for. I could have easily stayed in the pastoral position, even though it was forcing me into an environment and role that was inconsistent with who I am. I believe many discouraged pastors are actually in the wrong position or situation, but they've never been taught that there is more to ministry than just pastoring.

Way too many people don't step out towards their highest potential because they're afraid, but also because they don't love themselves. Their lack of self-love lulls them to make few gutsy decisions. They have little idea for who they are, so they give in to what other people want them to be. I could have remained stuck and angry if I was ok with status quo. Self-hate wanted to keep me there. Too often we want God to change something, but we're not willing to make the hard decision and take the risk.

I had to be willing to step out and the only way I could do that was to love myself enough to do so. I had to love myself into a decision that was right. That act of self-love involved stepping into the purpose that matched my identity and calling, not what people put on me.

There are many reading this who need to make the tough decision. They are hesitating, mostly because they do not love themselves enough. When you really love yourself, you gain astronomical courage to make choices that respect, honor and value who God made you to be. You see things better for yourself and your future.

Some reading this need to get out of a relationship, out of a job or even a church, but you haven't loved yourself to take that step. I am here as a testimony that in order to see change, you have to love yourself into it. I am committed to loving myself each day and never letting go of what I have experienced.

I am not going to beat myself up when things are not working out the way I thought they could. I refuse to let life tell me anything that God is not saying to me. My body is coming into more restoration and I am receiving the amazing effects that true self-love can bring. With this conviction, I am thrilled to inspire your own personal self-love revolution.

The frustrating thing about helping people with self-hate struggles is I cannot do the change for them. Only they can make that choice. I can set the perfect atmosphere of love over their life. I can pray, prophesy and love every cell in their being. But until they accept that and tell self-hatred to pack its bags, they will deflect the love that God sends to them.

You may be struggling with depression, bad habits or a toxic relationship you are stuck in. You may be overweight, ill or in a dead-end job and you need to make a decision for change. Many are going through troubling seasons. You're stuck, but you haven't loved yourself to make the strong decision for freedom and healing.

These times of struggle are when you need to be kind to yourself more than ever. Loathing the life you have does nothing to heal. Love is the answer, but if you wait for it to land on you, you may wait your whole life. It is important to say *yes* to love in your heart; possess it for yourself and walk into a better life.

I pray these words will instill courage within you to stand up and once for all, love who God made you to be and rip off those hindering chains that bind you. It's time you take back what was stolen from you and take some people with you!

So where do you need to love yourself into change?

QUESTIONS FOR CONSIDERATION

1. Why do you think that self-hate can be such a deceiving stronghold?

2. In what ways do you see self-hate manifesting the most in our world today?

3. What signs of self-hate hit home for you the most?

4. Where do you see it manifesting in your relationships? Passivity? Performance? Addictions?

5. What would it mean to love yourself in your current state?

6. What kind of decision do you need to make out of true love from God for yourself?

PRAYER

Father God, when I do not fully accept the love that you have for me, I recognize that I allow self-hate to creep in. I do not want to allow this villain to have a work in my life any longer. I recognize where I have had self-hate in my thoughts and have cooperated with not loving and accepting myself in the fullest dimension that God has planned for me. I repent of and renounce any participation with self-hate, stemming back from all previous generations. I ask forgiveness for having agreement with self-hate in my life and cooperating with it. I receive your forgiveness God and I forgive myself. I ask now that self-hate be broken and removed from my life. I command all thoughts, feelings and actions rooted in self-hate to be removed today in Jesus name. I cast down self-hate and receive the love my Father has for me today, in Jesus name, amen.

08

A Wonderfully Created Masterpiece

Your body hears everything your mind says.
- Naomi Judd

Take care of your body. It's the only place you have to live.
- Jim Rohn

The body appreciate it when we love ourselves. The benefits travel all the way down to a cellular level. Each body system works at its highest effectiveness when love is continually present within us. It can directly affect our physical health.

Every thought has a biological effect within the body. Our physiology was made to host a number of healthy thinking patterns. It can also handle temporary seasons of toxic thoughts, but it was never designed to carry the weight of chronic thinking that is destructive and resistant to love.

Depriving your body of love is like depriving it of food. You can get by without it for a little while, but as time passes, you feel the effects. Eventually, you can die. I believe many people pass away prematurely because love has not had a deep root in their life. The enemy knows if he can get us bound in self-defeating thinking patterns, he can compromise our health and wholeness in the long run.

Loving ourselves involves celebrating who we are, even down to our physical bodies. We were designed to love and cherish the body we were given. Each of us is unique in design, with no exact copy in existence. Every fingerprint is significant, specifically fashioned with an identity and purpose founded in the heart of God.

SELF-LOVE AND BODY IMAGE

We all have our flaws, but who's to say that one standard of beauty is the absolute and another isn't? Hundreds of years ago, during the Renaissance, a woman who was of fuller figure was considered an absolute beauty. Today it seems that beauty is relegated to a stick thin woman who has had procedures to alter her appearance. All of this to comply with an invisible standard that seems to grow more convoluted.

Body image struggles abound when we do not love ourselves. The enemy loves training people to possess a negative view of their appearance. This usually begins at the youngest of ages and becomes reinforced by certain relationships. If parents do not teach healthy self-image, the enemy has plenty to say that will bind children to negative body image thoughts.

Self-hate and self-rejection programs us to become professional critics of our own physical flaws. Magazines, television and online media perpetuate these ungodly perceptions, driving people to starve themselves or go through exercise roller coasters to gain a body one feels they can never attain. How often do we compare ourselves against images that are unrealistic and unhealthy?

Body image is a mental view we hold regarding our own physical appearance. We don't see what really is, but a trained perception. Our eyes focus on either admirable traits or flaws, the majority of humanity focusing on the flaws.

A lack of self-love will alter the way you see yourself. It will literally affect what your mind sees while you look in the mirror. Someone else could perceive you as beautiful, but it wouldn't matter. With self-rejecting tendencies, all you see is a magnified focus on whatever seems to be imperfect about you.

This negative self-image makes us uncomfortable in public settings. We feel uneasy in our own skin; living under constant reminders of being too fat, skinny, short or tall. Because of this, we cannot give ourselves fully to others because we are so preoccupied with our imperfections.

Despite what society attempts to do; no mode of Botox or cosmetic surgery will remedy the self-hate we carry. Most who get surgery or alterations end up needing more, simply because the root issue was never addressed. When we alter our bodies without ridding the self-hate that works against us, we in fact empower that mindset to dictate further decisions. The only remedy is loving ourselves, right where we are.

Body image comparison distracts our minds all day. Most of all, it takes the value away from the unique beauty we each possess. It also blocks us from connecting to the world with our true beauty.

Ironically, when we cannot connect to the beauty we possess, we often stop taking care of ourselves. We quit buying new clothes, getting our hair done and we let our weight get out of control. We stop caring, because we don't see value in ourselves anymore.

When my wife and I pray over a female, it is not uncommon for us to admonish her to treat herself to a facial, get her nails done or buy a pretty dress. Most would think that is not very spiritual, but in fact, it is. A woman blesses the world with her beauty if she is able to connect to that beauty within.

It is not just about looking beautiful on the outside, but radiating a beauty from the inside out. It is also a reminder to us of the glory of God. In fact, the Bible says, that a woman's hair is her glory[1]. Ever notice that when a woman loses her sense of worth one of the things she stops doing is getting her hair done? When you have a low self-image, doing simple things like caring for your body get put on the back shelf. The enemy is keen on stealing the woman's power by disconnecting her heart to an awareness of her personal beauty.

I have found that negative body image causes people to block love that is given to them. Women may struggle with intimacy in their marriage because of the negative feelings they carry about themselves. Men who struggle with their own toxic self-image will demand perfection in women, often nit-picking their wives' appearance. It will also drive them to obsess over their physiques at the gym, comparing themselves to other males and never feeling good enough.

Sometimes the most beautiful people can be deeply bound by

---

[1] 1 Corinthians 11:15

an unforgiving standard of perfection. No matter the attractiveness others see, they cannot see it themselves. That is why we cannot wait for someone to call us beautiful or handsome for us to connect to it. We must engage it from within by saying "yes" to who we are as God's creation.

THE SIGNIFICANCE OF OUR BIRTH

In 2001, God began to deal with how I saw myself by leading me to studying Psalm 139. I committed it to memorization, so as to embed the truth into my being. This Psalm is jam-packed with immense knowledge that God possess as well as His intimate involvement in my life. For me, it has been a game changer.

I have found there to be seven powerful precepts that will revolutionize how you see yourself and your existence on this planet. These statements have become guideposts in my heart to absorb God's love for me as His creation.

1. I became aware of God's presence and involvement in my conception. *For You formed my inward parts; You covered me in my mother's womb.* (Psalm 139:13)

I want to confront a lie up front that many people carry. The lie says, *you are a mistake. You are an accident. You are an inconvenience. No one notices you.* Lie! Lie! Lie! Some of you have carried this since you were born.

Before God even created the world, He knew you. Before you were ever conceived, God had an identity and calling in store for you. Not only that, God is personally and directly involved in your creation as a human being. The word "covered" means *to knit* and *to weave*. God covered you and intricately formed each thread of your biology.

God placed the responsibility of procreation on human beings, so all of us have been conceived under a variety of circumstances; some healthy, others not so much. Regardless of the circumstances surrounding your birth, God is intimately involved in the creation of who you are.

Does satan seek to interfere with this? Of course he does. Through mankind's choices and agreements with satan's lies, he gains access to steal, kill and destroy. Sometimes all he needs to do is create a story that God doesn't care and your birth is not special. The enemy is a thief, who loves to steal that from you in your life and journey.

When conception occurs, God breathes the breath of life. He involves Himself at a microscopic level, forming and fashioning the very cells of your being. He does only what an omniscient and omnipotent God could do by being personally connected to your formation.

Break the Lies by Saying Out Loud: *I am not a mistake. I am not an accident. I am not an inconvenience. God created me. I am significant. I am special in His eyes. God is aware of every part of my being. Thank you God for being involved in my conception and birth.*

2. I gained an amazement for God by understanding how amazing I am as His creation. *I will praise You, for I am fearfully and wonderfully made; marvelous are Your works, and that my soul knows very well.* (Psalm 139:14)

For most, this point can feel awkward; almost arrogant. It gets all our self-love struggles screaming inside of us. David, the writer of this Psalm is saying, *I praise You God...why? Because of what I see when I look at myself!*

To push this thought even further, when looking at himself, he says, *marvelous are your works!* What works are marvelous here? David's own physical body.

When was the last time you got a revelation of God by looking at yourself? Most people think this is preposterous. We have allowed religious conditioning to train us that we must reject ourselves in the act of praising God. This is foolishness.

We are not God, nor are we higher than God. We we're also not designed to celebrate ourselves apart from God. But there is something powerful that occurs within us when we joyously acknowledge God's amazing power to create us. David didn't have a microscope or science to impress him. He just looked at himself with his naked eye and gained a revelation of God's greatness!

Can you look in the mirror and say, *Wow! God is good!* For most people, their time in the mirror is the shortest moment of the day. They rush past it as quickly as possible; usually avoiding their own image for the rest of the day. We spend a lifetime criticizing and rejecting what we see. Each time we do that, we give the enemy power in our thoughts and we punish our physiology.

<u>Break the Lies by Saying Out Loud</u>: *I will not demean or devalue who I am as God's creation any longer. I choose to be excited over His design of me. It is exciting and fulfilling to rejoice over my creation. I will celebrate who God created me to be. I will look at myself in the mirror and celebrate what I see. God, I thank you for making me and forming me. I praise You because You made me!*

3. I began to tremble at the very thought of being created. *I am fearfully made.* (Psalm 139:14)

It was God's original design that when you see yourself, you would be amazed at how awesome He is. When we look at a beautiful painting, we celebrate the talented artist. Loving yourself in its truest form is not arrogance. It's celebrating how God made you. If we applaud a beautiful piece of art, we often say, "What a talented artist." The amazement at the work gives credit to the author of the work. When you celebrate who you are, you give praise to the One who made you.

A true understanding of God's power to create ought to make us tremble in our boots. The word *fearfully*, speaks of the fear of the Lord; an absolute awe and overwhelming encounter of glory. It involves an absolute astonishment of our Creator, who wants you to understand that His creation of you is a moment worth trembling in awe over.

So why do we compare ourselves or wish we were someone else, when there is great power covering our existence? Every time we crave to be someone else, we reject the awe of who we each are uniquely. When we become disconnected to how special we are, we lose sight of our significance on this planet. Yet when we get a glimpse of God's work over us, a fearful trembling hits our cells in astonishment. When that happens, nothing else matters.

Break the Lies by Saying Out Loud: *My creation is not an afterthought. My conception and birth are not something to gloss over. When God created me, it was a special occasion; a significant moment in history. I was made for a purpose greater than what I could even imagine. I choose to stand in awe and amazement over how God formed me.*

4. I saw myself as brilliantly set apart. *I am wonderfully made...* (Psalm 139:14)

There is a special wonder to your creation that is appointed to greatness. You are brilliant, unique and set aside for a beautiful purpose. No one can box you in or contain your potential. There is no equation or label that can cap the uniqueness of who you are.

God set you on an extraordinary pedestal, with an identity, anointing and destiny. It is not the same as the person next to you. No one can deposit on this planet what you were destined to contribute. God wants you to know He placed you on a special spot in His heart for divine impact.

<u>Break the Lies by Saying Out Loud</u>: *I break the lie that keeps me from believing that I am brilliant and unique in my design. I am set apart for a purpose. I am not on the back shelf. I am not forgotten. God knows me. He knows my name and every intricate part of my being. He has fashioned me to make a mark on this planet for His glory.*

5. I recognized my life as a marvelous work of God. *Marvelous are your works...* (Psalm 139:14)

This point is mute unless we connect to the meaning expressed here. *Marvelous* in the original language means:

- *A wonderful accomplishment that is difficult and hard to understand.*

- *To distinguish and separate as a wondrous action.*

- *Extraordinary and surpassing.*

Do you see yourself as God's extraordinary creation, surpassing any work humanity could come up with? Unfortunately, satan has been working for thousands of years to occlude humanity from seeing the divine power God possesses in creating us.

David looked at himself and said, "Marvelous are your works, God!" He was congratulating God on a "job well done" when he looked at his own physiology.

I learned a few years ago that how I interact with my physical appearance is a very important spiritual act. The more I compare or loathe how I look, the more I give the enemy room to speak and keep me bound in a knot that blocks love. When I rejoice over who God created me to be, I welcome the power of love to flood my body.

Break the Lies by Saying Out Loud: *I am significant! I am not an afterthought! My birth and creation are marvelous! I am a wondrous creation, an extraordinary manifestation. My birth shows the surpassing greatness of God, which cannot be understood with natural man's understanding.*

6. My conception was a secret place that only God and I share. *My frame was not hidden from You, when I was made in secret, and skillfully wrought in the lowest parts of the earth.* (Psalm 139:15) *You covered me in my mother's womb.* (Psalm 139:13)

Years ago, PBS aired a special on NOVA called "Life's Greatest Miracle[1]." In this fascinating presentation, they inserted a microscopic camera inside the womb of a female to

---

[1] http://www.pbs.org/wgbh/nova/body/life-greatest-miracle.html

record the process of conception in vivid detail. Beginning with the sperm fertilizing the egg, we are narrated through each developmental stage while the video footage unveils what humans for centuries were never able to see.

At the beginning of conception, human life is in a pre-embryonic state called a blastocyst. The sperm has fertilized the egg. Meanwhile God is breathing life and forming the intricate details of our human design. In this documentary, you can watch as the blastocyst travels in the womb to make its way into the uterine lining. When it leaves this stage, it is in a full embryonic state with many of the foundational settings in place. This includes blood, nerves, skeletal formations and more. But when it is tucked into the uterine lining, it moves into a hidden darkness, where the cameras can no longer see what is occurring at this stage.

Even though man has been able to develop advanced imaging to see into the inner workings of conception, there is a particular stage that cannot be seen with scientific tools. God knew that man would at some point be able to discover the inner workings of human anatomy, but He set this stage to be a hidden place—only visible to His eyes. For a moment, God blocks out the entire world, where He covers us in the womb and creates a secret place to set our framing and makeup.

David has a personal revelation regarding his conception that man cannot view with a microscope. There was a moment between him and His Creator that was incredibly precious and private. God literally created him in a private darkness, where no man could go. This is how amazing God is in His creation of you!

7. I realized that God has incredibly good thoughts towards me. *Your eyes saw my substance, being yet unformed. And in Your book they all were written, the days fashioned for me, when as yet there were none of them. How precious also are Your thoughts to me, O God! How great is the sum of them! If I should count them, they would be more in number than the sand; When I awake, I am still with You.* (Psalms 139:16-18)

God has a book, in which my life and purpose are written down. His everyday thoughts to me are not distant or angry, but precious. He looks at me with value and worth. If I begin experiencing His thoughts towards me, I could spend the rest of my life identifying them and still not reach all of them! They outnumber sand on the seashore. When I go to bed, He thinks about me. When I wake up, He's there watching me.

When we break into healthy self-love, we free ourselves to hear God's good thoughts towards us. We become empowered to receive from Him and experience how He thinks about us. We arm ourselves to engage God from the heart.

relationship with You God out of Your love, care and presence in my life!

YOU ARE GOD'S PRIZED DESIGN!

Ephesians 2:10 says, *we are His workmanship, created in Christ Jesus for good works, which God prepared beforehand that we should walk in them. Workmanship* is the Greek word *poiēma*, and it speaks of *a fabric or that which is made, from a creator*. When God looks at you, He sees you as a mighty work; a work of His hands!

Notice that *we* are the workmanship. We were created with an identity of being God's special creation—His masterpiece. When we get a hold of the masterpiece that we are, we align ourselves into the calling He has given us.

We were *created for good works*. When we are solid in our identity, our works flow powerfully out of that. So many people are working tirelessly for an identity. What they need to do is connect to the identity they have already and let their work flow out of that.

I have found that so many do not set out to do great things because they do not see themselves as great. Or they may attempt to do works with the hope that they will feel great someday. Both mindsets are unhealthy. God designed for us to see His greatness on the inside of us so we can live out our daily purpose from a powerful identity.

YOUR HEALTH DEPENDS ON IT

The inner workings of your body erode when love is absent. This is because your body was never made to live without love. It was uniquely designed to live in the electro-chemical signals that love carries. Science is even proving that a healthy self-image, strong relationships and stable self-love are helpful ingredients towards overall health and vitality.

It is a biological fact that people who do not feel good about themselves can develop low serotonin levels, have poor immune systems, develop chronic health issues, have continual relationship struggles and develop addictive patterns. Your body will respond to the toxic thoughts at work within you. We were never made to live in chronic states of fear, insecurity, self-rejection, self-hatred or any other form of self-conflicting battles. The enemy knows that if his ways of thinking are kept in our lives, he can steal and destroy our health, all from the lack of self-love operating in our lives.

LOVING YOUR TEMPLE

Every one of us lives in a temporary body, which the Bible calls the temple of the Holy Spirit. Although this current body is temporary, it is still of value, for it houses the work that God chooses to do through you in this lifetime. How you treat your temple has a direct effect on how well the inner man can manifest.

For this is the will of God, your sanctification: that you should abstain from sexual immorality; that each of you should know how to possess his own vessel in sanctification and honor.[1]

The exhortation in this verse is to honor our bodies by not engaging in sexual immorality, for it violates the bodies God created them with. Loving ourselves means saving our sexuality for the context God design it to live in. But even further, learning to love one's self involves learning how to honor your body in day-to-day decisions.

Sanctification is the process of being set apart from sin. How many times do we give into a sinful mindset by: a) rejecting the body God gave us, b) not caring for and honoring the body we have. The sin that needs to be removed from our lives is the sin of not loving ourselves.

One of the biggest ways we can manifest freedom from self-love struggles is by showing honor and care to our physical body. Sometimes the most spiritual act you can do is eat well, go exercise, take a nap or get care. Honoring our bodies is a high level of self-love; which lines up with how God sees us.

A lack of self-love conditions masses of people to stop taking care of themselves. They no longer update their hairstyle and discontinue getting new clothes. They often write it off to "I don't have time" or "I'm saving money." When the reality is at some point they simply lost a connection to loving themselves or they never had it at all to begin with. I noticed that when I was down on myself or not in a self-love posture, I stopped feeding healthy habits and caring for myself as much.

I never give my wife a hard time about getting her hair done. I even encourage her to get her nails done and get whatever

---

[1] 1 Thessalonians 4:3-4

beauty aids she needs. Why? I want her to feel beautiful about herself. I am willing to make whatever financial sacrifices necessary to make sure of that, because I understand the connection between self-love and self-care.

BREAKING OFF THE CHAINS

I remember when I was little; I had a much bigger head than other kids. My doctor was even concerned as a child that something may be wrong, so they had to monitor my growth to ensure that my development was on track. In school, kids would make fun of me and call me names. I was always humiliated to wear a fitted ball cap because they rarely had my size. When I was in a young men's ranger group, my dad had to custom sew a beret for me so that it would fit my larger head.

I used to hate the size of my head, its shape and look. Therefore, I ignored my reflection in the mirror as much as possible. But as I got more free to love myself, how big my head was just disappeared into the background. It no longer became a focus. I can look more freely at myself and appreciate my design, with flaws included. I notice the more I do that, the more handsome I actually feel. My wife notices it more and more as she feels the confidence manifesting from me. It's not arrogance. If you know my story, you will know it is a work of the Spirit of God. Sometimes the most powerful step towards loving yourself can occur by coming into agreement over the beauty of who you are as God's creation.

QUESTIONS FOR CONSIDERATION:

1. Where have you seen body image issues manifest the most? In your life and those around you?

2. Of the seven insights from Psalm 139 given, which one touched your heart the most?

3. When you realize that your creation was a private moment between you and Father God, how does your heart respond to this?

4. How was your birth experience? What were the circumstances surrounding your conception and birth? Is it possible that God may need to heal that experience?

5. In what way can you begin loving and accepting who you are as God's creation today?

6. How can you begin to help others love and accept their own physical body and appearance?

PRAYER

Father God, I thank you today that I am your wonderful creation. When I look at myself, I want to see the beauty and power of who you are. I ask that You help me to gain an image of what You see, so that I can appreciate how You made me to be. I bless my conception. I recognize that before I was even born, You knew me. You fashioned me for a purpose. You set me on this planet to walk in greatness. I am not a mistake. I am not an inconvenience. I bless my birth. I break off any attacks over my delivery as a baby, my mother's pregnancy and any negative situations surrounding my birth. No matter what my father and mother have or have not done, God You created me to be Your creation; Your special creation. I am loved by You. I am accepted by You. I am significant. I am fashioned and designed for an eternal purpose. So today, I come into greater agreement with how precious You have made me to be. I see in my creation, the greatness of who You are.

09

The Monster We Must All Confront

Self-pity is easily the most destructive of non-pharmaceutical narcotics. It is addictive and separates the victim from reality.
- John W. Gardner

There is a key threshold to cross in order to move from being empty of self-love and into the freedom of experiencing God's love for ourselves. Each of us will have to face an enemy that has embedded itself into the fibers of our thinking. Because of not being loved properly, masses of people have developed a coping mechanism that keeps them from tasting freedom. It's the victim posture of self-pity.

All of us have victim ways of thinking that spring up. We approach life in certain areas as, *happening to us*, instead of *us happening to life*. We connect our success and breakthrough to how well circumstances work for us, instead of focusing on just living as an overcomer in all things.

For years, I have been working with people who have deep

issues regarding self-image, self-love and relationship hurts. They rejoice when they see what I teach and the heart of love I seek to deliver in all things. Yet there is a certain point in time where love calls them to take responsibility for their lives and press forward into healed territory. This is a critical threshold, where God seeks to move us from victims to victors.

This is not a step that someone can take for us, but only one that we can make by our own choice. God Himself cannot and will not force this upon us. It is an invitation, but we must reserve our own spot in the army of overcomers.

If a person does not cross this threshold by becoming an overcomer, they can become entrenched in a victim mindset. They can develop an anger at life, others and God, blaming them for their own lack of progress. Some will lash back harshly, claiming everyone is against them; that God Himself does not care. Just when massive breakthrough is about to happen, satan pulls the pity card to keep people trapped in a victim way of living. They can lash out at those who actually love them the most, those who are not putting up with the pity talk.

A MAJOR SHIFT IN LIVING

Most people do not realize they live as victims. They don't see that self-pity is their "go to" response for difficult days and challenges. They are so accustomed to seeing circumstances as being the problem; they never rise to the next level. They fail to see that change needs to happen internally, before we can see it manifest externally.

Our circumstances actually reveal where we need to grow.

They confront our weaknesses and vulnerabilities. They seep through the cracks of our foundation, tearing away at areas where our faith is weak. This is an assignment of the enemy to steal, kill and destroy, but it can be a godly invitation to grow into what we have not yet manifested.

If we don't make the change into a victorious mindset, we will become used to defeated living and fail to take personal responsibility. Trials and hardships will own us, rather than become incubators for our growth propulsion.

Self-pity is a monster, but it works hard to hide without detection. It acts as the quicksand of hell to keep us sinking into our problems with no resolve. It presents itself as self-compassion, when really it is self-hate's greatest friend. It keeps you in a victim posture, believing there is no hope for change. It's a hook that takes millions of people out daily, keeping them locked in a victimization. When we come into agreement with this mindset, we always look for someone to rescue us, rather than becoming empowered to step out and rescue ourselves.

EARLY TRAINING

I developed a victim mentality very early in life. It presented itself as soon as I can remember. My earliest memories of pain and hardship were marked with me responding as a victim. I would sit in beautiful one-man pity party. All I was thinking was, "If I do this, someone will come and rescue me." I thought that God or someone would see my blatant need for help and respond to rescue me out of my pain.

This is sometimes embarrassing to think about, but I used

pity on my parents, coaches, teachers and leaders. It was a manipulation on people's emotions to gain sympathy and remove myself from any challenges. It took a great deal of honesty and courage to face this and make the transition into stronger patterns.

In raising our children, we are working hard to equip them to live as overcomers. We've taught them to differentiate between crying over genuine pain and crying "pity tears." The earlier they can identify this, the better they will be able to process pain, yet position themselves to live victorious.

Unfortunately, we usually need someone to call us out on our pity and victim behavior. It can be so excruciating to be on the receiving end of this. Trust me. I've had to be called out on it a number of times. Too often we just want to sit and feel sorry for ourselves. But the more I grow, the more God says, "Enough is enough. Get up soldier and kick out the enemy!"

Quite often, people in self-pity and victim mindsets need a loving intervention to wake them out of their victimized posture. Only those who really want transformation will respond to the rebuke and grow. When we move into becoming victors and overcomers, the whole game changes, because we disempower the enemy. I have found it to be one of the most healing and transformative changes I know of.

SELF-PITY'S RESPONSE

One of the greatest manifestations of victim thinking and self-pity is the "shutdown" response. When someone shuts down, they have hit the emotional limit of what they think they can handle. They may be physically present in the room, but they have emotionally shut down from engaging people and life. It's satan's way of escape for us. We feel there's nothing else we can do, so we disconnect relationally and delve into an internal world.

People shut down when they feel they have hit their emotional limit. The challenges they face are actually an opportunity to press in further and find the jewel of growth. Yet most miss it because they disengage and shut themselves off from what is available.

It's ok to ask for an emotional break, so one can think things over and respond in a healthy way. But it is an entirely different thing to disengage from working things out. I have watched hundreds of people shut down, just before an amazing breakthrough was about to open up.

Why do we do this? It's often because we have no training on how to engage hard experiences. We lack the mentoring on how to process pain, yet also work toward overcoming. In order to change, many people have to dig deep for something they don't have a clear reference for. They have been so conditioned to let life happen to them, they lack the vision for conquering. We quit just when we have a chance to go to a new level.

In our greatest challenges, when we feel we cannot take it anymore, this is where we can learn to grow the most. We recognize we were not loved or helped in the way that we needed. We allow ourselves to weep, grieve and let God have access to our broken hearts. But we don't remain in this condition. Self-pity and victim thinking want to keep us there, using every disappointment and roadblock as ammunition that things will never change.

We cannot expect others to move us into the overcomer's mindset. Not even God can do that without our permission. He will work alongside our personal agreement with His power that lives within us. Faith looks for every opportunity to overcome. Unbelief tells us to stay in pity because nothing will change.

TEARING DOWN THE WALLS

Pride will keep self-pity intact. In fact, self-pity is actually a form of pride, for it bucks personal responsibility to overcome. It resists true love and denies the good future God has for you.

In Isaiah 45:9, we see how pride bucks the love and design of God, where the prophet says, *Shall the clay say to him who forms it, 'What are you making?'*

The enemy will train us to stay in our junk and deem it acceptable to soak in emotional sewage. It will keep us stubborn and unwilling to even look in the mirror and love ourselves. The moment someone speaks the truth in love, something will rise up in you, causing you to think, "they don't love me!" Self-pity will not allow us to be corrected in our junk. It will say that someone who loves us enough to bring correction is mean and hateful.

Unfortunately, this keeps our families, churches and friendships at a surface level. No one has permission to speak the straight truth in love without someone withdrawing and cutting off relationship. When we break self-pity and victim thinking, we learn to love correction, for in it, our journey is enhanced and strengthened.

ISOLATION

Self-pity's tactic is to move us into emotional isolation, where the enemy's sniper can easily take us out. When we are in community, it's much harder for the enemy to have his way. In isolation, we become a standard to ourselves, not learning or growing from the input and wisdom of others. We remove ourselves from authority figures and people that will challenge us to grow.

Don't mistake isolation from solitude. Solitude is getting alone with yourself or with God, the goal being refreshment. Jesus lived out the daily practice of solitude. When we engage solitude, it empowers us to interact with others in a more refreshed posture.

Isolation may appear as solitude, but it causes us to withdraw from people out of hurt. We avoid others. Isolation trains us to withdraw from relationships.

Married couples can battle this. Two people can be living in the same home and one is isolated from the other. The enemy knows if he can get couples emotionally separated then they lose their power to live as one.

Many believers live very isolated lives. They have been hurt so badly that they cannot see the point to remaining in fellowship.

I get it. People out there are becoming more and more dangerous in their approach. They can be with you one moment and betray you the next. Yet this cannot be an excuse to remove ourselves from humanity. God cannot use us if we are isolated from the very people He wants us to touch. When relationships get tough, the enemy will convince us to isolate. Usually the best thing to do is the opposite.

In Hebrews 10:25 it tells us to not forsake the assembling of ourselves together. It's important that as a part of your healing journey, you participate in regular gatherings with those you can feel safe with; those who know you but also partner with your potential. You cannot do this alone. We all need to cultivate a tribe around us that can love, sharpen and support our overcoming.

INTROSPECTION

If you have any self-love battles, odds are you may need to kick the introspection habit; the enemy's counterfeit to mature self-awareness and discernment. Constant introspection is a bad habit of obsessively analyzing ourselves with the hopes we will someday find the answer we need to move forward.

Introspection causes us to navel-gaze daily. We lose sight of the world around us and the difference love can make working through us. We're so obsessed about our pain and struggle; we fail to see others or the world around.

Introspection as a continual habit is not helpful. As you recognize your battles; you will have to develop a front forward mindset. The rear view mirror needs to be small and your front window large. The main focus cannot be on the past, but the present that is in front of you.

Introspection won't let that happen. It keeps us distracted; focusing on our present pain and past heartache. We become so mindful of ourselves we spend more time looking at how we feel, so we self-analyze all day. We can't engage, because we are stuck in ourselves. It makes others want to smack us out of it.

God wants to engage us at a heart level, but too many are so distracted in their thoughts they can't engage His affection. We spend so much time thinking and analyzing our thoughts and lives that we never live. We never just get out there and let go. In order to break self-love battles, we're going to have to let go and let God plant a kiss of affection over us.

BELIEVING IN LOVE

When we come into the love of God, we do so with belief from the heart. We embrace what God says and overcome the resistance that bucks His love and affection for us. I cannot expect God to heal my life if I continue tolerating unbelief regarding God's ability to work in my life. In order to engage the fullest power of God's love, I have to increase my muscles of belief.

If I were to define unbelief, it would be *an atmosphere of thought where we refuse to be persuaded*. It's a haze that clouds our vision to believe and walk in powerful faith. Because of it, many people do not enter the rest of what God says. They wander in their junk and never settle.

Unbelief seeks to keep us from having an inner agreement with God's love. The resistance wins every time. Unbelief covers the thinking of our modern culture, keeping people from seeing beyond what is in front of them. We even miss the very love of God that is invading our lives because unbelief blocks it.

Unbelief is the cornerstone of satan's operation. It is infused into the fiber of every stronghold he seeks to establish. All of us have our battles of unbelief. They are usually tied to a disappointment, a hurt or simple lack of faith references. In order to break free, we have to cast down the work of unbelief, so we can choose to rest in the power of God's love. Remember, love believes all things[1]. When love is present, it carries the ability to believe for anything, even the most seemingly impossible.

QUESTIONS FOR CONSIDERATION

1. Where do you find yourself coming into agreement with a self-pity mindset?

2. Why do people shut down emotionally, especially in moments where they may have a chance to grow to a new level in their life?

3. What are some ways that we can isolate in our junk?

4. Where do you need to take responsibility and make a strong decision to live as an overcomer? What step do you need to take today?

5. Do you find patterns where you get so deep in your own thoughts that you fall into introspection? What are some ways you can break those patterns?

6. In what way does unbelief seek to block your ability to walk in love from God towards yourself?

---

[1] 1 Corinthians 13:7

PRAYER

Father God, I recognize where the victim mindset and self-pity have become a way of life in my thinking. The battles I have faced and the brokenness I struggle with have become prisons around me, keeping me from seeing the hope you have for my life. I do not want to be chained to my limitations or difficulties any longer.

Today, I do what no one else can do for me: I take responsibility for my freedom. I take my place as a child of God today to stand for my healing and my deliverance. I repent and I renounce victimization. I repent and I renounce self-pity. I command the works of those mindsets to be gone in the name of Jesus.

Today I give thanks for who God is. I declare that He is a good God. He is a good Father. I declare today that I am a child of God who is deeply loved by Him. I have what it takes in Christ Jesus to overcome and break free from the chains that bind me. I declare today that I will no longer be a victim. I am not a victim any longer.

I will no longer use self-loathing, self-pity or hopelessness as a way of coping with my problems. I refuse to "check-out" of life and miss out on the victories I can participate in. I command all works of oppression, heaviness and discouragement that keep self-pity in place to leave in Jesus name. I am loved. I will love myself. I will love myself into freedom. I am not a victim. I am victorious! God is with me and will empower me to break free from every chain! I declare that I am taking my life back! In Jesus' name. Amen.

10

Using Your Rudder

But if thought corrupts language, language can also corrupt thought.
— George Orwell, 1984

I am going to share with you one of the most effective habits in my life. It has revolutionized how I heal, overcome struggles and shift my perspective. I can literally change my spiritual and emotional state within minutes because of what I practice in the pages of this chapter. It is incredibly simple yet mostly underutilized.

In order to free ourselves, we have to gain a heart connection to love. Most claim to know what love is, but few seem to walk in the great power of it. There has to be a personal impact of love.

How do we know that we carry a healthy possession of love in our lives? When we become comfortable with loving and being loved authentically, that's a good sign. When love has an impact on how we think, how we do relationships and how we process life emotionally, we are moving in the right direction. When our inner arguments over our self-image, appearance and insecurities begin to lose their volume, self-love is having its work.

Although reading about self-love is important, we have to process it out in real life. Love must have its work into our belief system, where we are impacted down to the marrow of our bones. True belief means there is an inner unity to what God says. If we feel constant resistance, that's the enemy's programming.

But how do you begin moving forward in self-love when the whole concept feels so foreign? With very few models out there, how can we create new habits and steps of faith that welcome God's love to penetrate our hearts?

DIGGING DEEPER

I have worked with people for decades and have crossed paths with thousands of people who have this love deficit issue. They recognize their brokenness and need for love, but don't know how to move towards healthy love. Speakers and teachers will say, "You need to receive God's love. Let God love you" yet everyone has this inner cry saying, "Yeah, but how?"

Most go further into discouragement by thinking, "something is just wrong with me." They fall into the darkness of accusation the enemy is perpetrating to keep them feeling disqualified and defeated.

People from all over have contacted me over this issue. The dilemma caused me to go into the spiritual laboratory with God. I began to seek Him with tenacity over this issue. "God, why is it we don't know how to be loved and love ourselves?" What are we to do about this?

I learned that we need two main things. **First, we need solid discernment;** the ability to see the thoughts and emotions that block the flow of love, as not their truest self, but from the enemy. So much of our thoughts and impressions flood through us without any awareness. I knew I needed to help awaken people to the spiritual battle.

Second, we need action steps. I believe in being highly spiritual, yet extremely practical; where the precepts of the Kingdom of God can take shape in our daily life. People don't have a great deal of references for healthy love, so we need a grid to walk this thing out.

If spiritual precepts taught do not have actionable manifestations, what we learn goes dormant. The ultimate manifestation of God lies in how our actions and relationships change.

MOUTH TO HEART

We have to awaken the heart to what loving ourselves means. The heart has to come alive to be able to identify love and walk effectively in it.

I have found that one of the greatest ways to break open the life of the heart is through the power of words. Being around people who speak words of life is helpful, but you cannot rely on people to be your source. You have to learn how to speak life giving words to yourself.

Your mouth is a rudder[1], meaning your words have the

---

[1] James 3:4-5

capacity to steer your heart into specific directions. It's important we know how to use our words to jumpstart our heart and come alive to loving ourselves.

The life of the heart is connected to our mouth and words. What we speak has a connection to what's going on within. The New Testament is covered with teachings that emphasize the connection of the heart to the mouth.

A good man out of the good treasure of his heart brings forth good; and an evil man out of the evil treasure of his heart brings forth evil. For out of the abundance of the heart his mouth speaks. Luke 6:45

For assuredly, I say to you, whoever says to this mountain, 'Be removed and be cast into the sea,' and does not doubt in his heart, but believes that those things he says will be done, he will have whatever he says. Mark 11:23

THE MISSING LINK

So here is the key that we need to activate. When we think of the heart connection, we typically emphasize the heart believing something then speaking it. The common flow becomes believe it first, then say it. The problem is we can develop a limiting mindset which says, "I won't say it until I really believe it."

I lived for years thinking; "I can't say that just yet, because I do not fully believe it in my heart. I don't want to be a hypocrite." This mindset subtly blocked me from making progress in areas I was trapped in. You do not need to fully believe something to start speaking it. Like the father in Mark 9:24, we can say, "I believe, but help me with my unbelief!"

To jump start our hearts into love, the biggest thing we can do is utilize our words to speak life and love over it. Words are so powerful that they can take a dead heart and bring life to it. They can resurrect lost hope, heal broken hearts and release change in the midst of impossibilities.

Sometimes I tell people, "it's ok to somewhat fake it until you make it." All you need is a "want to." You may struggle to love yourself, but do you want to? If the answer is *yes*, then you need to begin using your words to open up love in your heart.

DEATH TALK

The biggest way we can monitor our capacity to live in self-love is by examining how we talk about ourselves. Every day, most people cap their own potential by what comes out of their own mouth. They point out every flaw they have with contempt and spew unbelief over their circumstances. Negativity surrounds us. Social media pages and blogs are riddled with negatively based words that keep people in a pessimistic prison.

I watch it over and over. People talk so negatively about themselves; their lives and their circumstances. It has become a social norm. Try saying nothing negative for 30 days and you will see how much it's a part of our life. We've become used to living with this cloud over our existence.

We cannot move into loving ourselves unless we change our words. They can no longer be filled with negativity, self-hate and self-rejection, while we wonder why we can't seem to break free. The enemy gains fuel off of our negative words. He also gains momentum from our silence, where we should talk, but don't.

We sit passively when we should be actively speaking life.

During a particularly rough season of my life, where my physical health was not strong, my energy was weak and my circumstances seemed impossible, I had to confront my words in a dynamic way. I felt myself emotionally drowning, where nothing seemed to break free and my situation was not changing. It was in this deep season of darkness that I began to understand how to love myself with my words.

In the midst of this trying season, I realized the greatest thing I needed to do was be kind to myself. To add to the already difficult situation with being hard on myself and unkind with negative words was doing me no good. So I decided to leverage my words in the power of God's love over my life. I made the decision that I was going to be kind to myself, no matter what I was going through. I also decided I was going to be patient with my process and myself.

Patience and kindness are the pillars of love, so walking in them welcomes love. There is no better way to exercise patience and kindness than to engage them with our words.

With much trial and error, I began to use my words every day to add power to my overcoming journey. I literally spoke myself into self-love and talked myself into life. I used words to turn the tables on the enemy.

GETTING INTO STILLNESS

I am going to share with you what I began to practice. It is something I now utilize on a daily basis. Step by step, I will instruct you how to position yourself for love by using your words with greater power. For some this might feel weird, because we are used to living in toxic patterns and not slowing down to deal with our hearts.

But if you engage this process, you will see change. I have never worked with anyone who did not see fruit from daily practicing this process.

You'll need to do this every day. You cannot skip a day. As much as you need air, food and water, you need to practice these exercises as though your life depends on it.

The first thing you are going to have to do is learn to get quiet. For most, this can seem like a daunting task, but it's one that you need if you want to walk in the healing power of self-love. A hurried life works counter cultural to love. Stillness, rest and a listening heart is the recipe for engaging more of God's love.

Find a quiet place where you are not going to be distracted. Turn off any television, computers or phone alerts. You want to quiet yourself, so as to access love in your heart. But we first want to access more of God's peace, so love can rest deeper. This is the art of what the Bible calls being still and knowing[1]—the ability to sit and *BE,* with no agenda or racing thoughts. Just relationship with God.

Determine how long you want to practice this silence. If you have never done this, I recommend only five minutes. Most people feel like they are going to die sitting in only five to ten minutes of silence.

---

[1] Psalm 46:10

Don't overwhelm yourself and don't get upset because you can't last very long, that's not loving to yourself. Start somewhere and grow from there. I started with 1 minute, because that was all I could do. Now I can sit in silence as long as I need to, but it took some practice. So be encouraged. You can do this.

You may need to set a timer, so this time is focused and intentional. **Second, place your hand over your heart.** That's a cue for your heart to receive what you are engaging. Close your eyes. Let your mind calm down from constant wandering and settle into peace. Don't feel the need to pray, because that can lead you into racing thoughts and endless things you want to say to God. You can certainly pray, but I want you to learn how to receive. This time is designed for you to build those receiving muscles, so love can land more freely. This will actually empower your prayer life much more.

Third, take in deep breaths. Take slow and deep breaths, calming your body and positioning yourself to enter into a restful position. Set your attention on learning to receive from God. We do this by focusing our thoughts on who He is without getting into racing specifics. Focus on His goodness and faithfulness with gratitude. Let your heart engage these thoughts to prepare yourself to receive love, as you have your hand over your heart.

When I find my mind wandering, I focus back on taking in deep breaths. Remember, breath in the Bible is *pneuma*, the word translated *spirit*. We are breathing in the Spirit of God and breathing out toxicity. Most important, keep it simple.

If you find your mind all over the place, don't worry. This is normal. In love, bring those thoughts back in and let peace settle into your heart. If you can go longer than the time allotted, by all means do it. The longer you can sit in stillness, the better.

LOVING SELF-TALK

Once you are still, you will need to use your words for awakening your heart to self-love. This is very simple. In the practice of stillness and peace, you are going to say these three simple declarations. Write them down on a card or on your phone so you are reminded to say them over and over; not only in this moment, but all throughout the day. As you take in deep breaths, say these words to yourself calmly and confidently.

God loves me.

I love myself.

I have what it takes to overcome.

Say them slowly and intentionally. Don't race through this at all. Extract every bit of meaning from these sentences. Repeat them over and over to let the meaning sink in. Let the power of the words penetrate your being.

Breathe in and out as you say them. Slowly repeat these three sentences over and over again until you are focusing completely on what they mean. This is actually what biblical meditation is—muttering a certain thought over and over until it becomes engrafted into the fiber of our being.

I recommend starting every day and ending every day this way. If you are just starting off, do this in your 5-10 minutes of silence before you go about your day. As you speak these words, let your mind see how love can affect your entire life, your health, your relationships, your decisions and your walk with God.

These three sentences are addressing three keys to moving

into healthy self-love. The first statement brings agreement to the love God has for you. The second sentence declares an agreement for you to receive that love for yourself. The third statement breaks the power of victim thinking that has convinced you that you are trapped or limited.

As you grow in these statements, you can add declarations to this list. At the time of this writing, my daily list has grown to about 30 declarations. I do not recommend starting off that way, because it can be challenging to connect to 30 statements off the jump. Starting small helps you focus more simply. Over time you can add statements that speak to an overcoming of certain strongholds you deal with:

I love my life

I am strong

I have value

I have worth

I have a good future

My negative past will not be my future

As you become used to this practice, you can add declarations that speak to who you are and your future.

Some people write this off as a *"name it and claim it"* thing. Others feel really awkward even applying this process. It can also be easy to write this off as self-help mumbo jumbo. Yet we can no longer dismiss the truth that God created our words to be extremely powerful. Don't let the enemy steal it from you.

Practicing healthy declarations involves coming into agreement with what God says about you and your life. Speaking it out loud jumpstarts the power of our hearts. This is our opportunity to become one with the Word of God by using our words to align our agreement with Him.

When should we stop saying these words? Never. They need to become a part of our life and belief system. Until we get into complete inner unity with the truth of God's words over our life, we have to tenaciously declare these statements over and over.

You may feel a great deal of resistance. This is ok. Most people hit a wall when they say, "I love myself." Don't be afraid of it, nor bask in the negativity that rises up. You are going to move past it, so develop your focus into the new way. Don't get discouraged if it doesn't click in overnight.

So to sum it up:

1. Write these declarations down.

2. Say them every day.

3. Say them until you believe them.

4. Don't ever stop. Ever.

THE POWER OF MIRROR TALK

Since most of us went through life never hearing how beautiful or handsome we were, it's important to rewire our thinking and establish new patterns of how we see ourselves. This leads us to another empowering habit; one that I call "mirror talk."

In this exercise, you get in front of a mirror and look at yourself in the eyes. This is not a time to focus on your flaws, but to connect to how God sees you. Glancing in the mirror and rushing away does no good. We are going to train ourselves to begin liking what we see. You are going to face yourself, so that you can love yourself.

While looking in the mirror, take a moment to engage yourself in the eyes. You can do this in any mirror, even the rearview mirror of your car, but find a place where you can settle for a minute. As you face yourself, the goal is to release kindness with your words, while you connect them with your eyes. So while looking into your own eyes, begin to say these words out loud to yourself.

God loves me.

I love myself.

You have what it takes to overcome.

(Your Name), you are loved.

You are handsome (For males)

You are beautiful. (For females)

You are a man (or woman) of God.

You are valued.

You are loved.

You are worth being loved.

We all know that looking into someone's eyes is a step towards connection. Therefore, looking into your own eyes is an opportunity to minister to yourself; allowing what God says to flow into your being.

This particular exercise can be very uncomfortable for many, who have become so used to beating themselves up, criticizing their looks and avoiding the sight of themselves all together. We submerge into parenting, work or others roles, while losing who we really are at the core. These exercises bring us back to our true self as God's children, apart from all our daily roles. At the end of the day, my identity is not in my roles, but in being God's kid. I am a loved child of God.

How do I grow as God's child? By looking in His mirror and seeing what He sees. If I see what He sees, I will act out of the identity I have connected to. Every person on this planet lives out of how they see themselves. Taking time to look in the mirror and cultivate a God perspective on our lives not only drives out self-battles, it moves us into greater growth in who we are.

DEVELOPING PERSONAL DECLARATIONS

As you get used to speaking over yourself, your written and spoken words will increase. On a daily basis, my personal declarations can include anywhere from 40 to 100 statements I am embedding into my being. This is a far cry from my days of saying nothing over myself and just getting by from day to day. I lived most of my life in reactionary mode, responding to daily crisis. Today, I set the stage of what I am going to think on and where I set my affection. What a greater place to live!

Overtime, you'll find new statements to add. You can add declarations that address the particular battles you face. Here are a number of examples:

I accept myself right where I am.

I have nothing to prove today.

I am safe today.

I have the ability to give and receive affection.

What other people think of me does not rule me.

Opportunities are coming my way.

I am becoming fear free.

Addictions are leaving me today.

Key relationships are arriving to me, right on time.

There is no pressure.

I am grateful.

In fact, I not only do this myself, my family practices this each day. On the ride to school, we walk our children through a series of declarations we have taught them; powerful statements that remind them of who they are and how much they are loved. We make it fun and exciting, so they will engage it with their hearts. We say things together like:

I am smart!

I am brave!

I am an overcomer!

Dad loves me. Mom loves me.

God loves me and I love myself!

And we like to end our family declarations with a fun little...

And the DeJesus' rock!

REVEALED IN PRAYER LIFE

The more I cultivate declarations, the more my prayer life improves. I spend more time praying like a son, rather than a slave. A slave spends prayer time asking, begging and pleading with God. A son spends more time connecting to God's heart, declaring who God is and expressing gratitude for what God is doing.

I spend a lot less time asking and more time declaring God's heart over my life. I bless people I interact with. I declare blessing over businesses I engage, stores I walk into and people I interact with.

I become a thermostat rather than a thermometer. A thermometer just knows how to read the temperature, which is easy for anyone to do. A thermostat knows how to set the spiritual temperature in a giving environment. One of the biggest ways we can do this is to use the power of declaration in everything we do.

Our words can release so much life into others. But we must give out what we are harvesting in ourselves. A much better way to live is to share what you have been cultivating and receiving. Give out to others what you are marinating in your own personal life. You don't have to arrive to do this, just give out from where you are headed.

QUESTIONS FOR CONSIDERATION

1. Where have you noticed words you speak that are negative and keep you from walking in love towards yourself?

2. Where have you neglected to speak life and love over yourself?

3. What is the one statement you could begin saying every day that would be effective for your growth?

4. Take a moment to sit down and write the first few declarations. Then begin to add a couple to that list that are custom made for you. Set a time every day that you will speak them out loud.

PRAYER

Father, I realize that You created words to be powerful and transformational. You created the world with spoken words and You created me to use my words to breathe life into every situation. I open my heart today to receive more of your love by coming into agreement with love in my words. Today, I declare that I am loved, accepted and approved of by You. You love me, You are proud of me and You are with me. I love You God. I love myself today. I love and accept myself with the love You have for me Father. I declare today that I will love myself. No longer will I accept the counterfeit. I am free to love and be loved in Jesus name!

11

Taking Action
Key Steps for Loving Yourself

Being loved and walking that out is a daily process, so you are going to need some tools to overcome for loving yourself. Because love affects everything in life, you need to have an "all hands on deck" approach. You cannot expect to break through and live half-hearted with this battle. Freedom has to be desired more than anything. Living in the fullness of love is the greatest blessing anyone can possess.

If you're looking for an easy way or quick pill to freedom, expect to be disappointed. You may end up quitting and going back to familiar ways very quickly. You have to hunger and desire for it more than comfort, ease or status quo. No one can want it more than you do. A deep fire has to burn within to live free and love yourself. Otherwise this process will be frustrating. But if you want an overcomer's heart, be willing to do what needs to be done in order to live a life of healthy love.

It is possible to be free. I have experienced it and many I have worked with have rejoiced in the clean air of freedom. We just need to be willing to make the investment.

I love going into deep spiritual precepts, but I also love the practical day-to-day habits that add to the reservoir of victory. In these next pages, I want to outline some key mindsets and practices that will in the long term, equip you into knowing what it means to be a loved child of God.

1. Make a firm decision that you are going to do whatever it takes to live free in loving yourself. I believe this is the most critical step, because most people are one strong decision away from everything changing. When we make a firm decision, we draw a line in the sand and refuse to ever go back.

Sometimes the pain of not changing needs to intensify so much that you realize you *must* change. Making the decision to change, no matter what, moves us from living as victims to taking on the mindset of an overcomer. Victims always think they don't have a choice regarding their life, whereas overcomers know they have the ability to make a decision to grow despite circumstances. No matter what others do or your life situation, making the decision to love yourself is one hundred percent up to you.

2. Fight the enemy, not yourself. Satan and his army is the enemy; you are not. Stop believing the lie, because it is one of satan's biggest traps. It is important to separate these toxic thoughts as "not you." Otherwise you will go with the destructive impulses without any idea you are being deceived. Once you begin to separate these thoughts as not being your own, but from the enemy, two great things can happen.

One is, you will learn to stop beating yourself up. Second, you will gain more leverage on your battles. You will more clearly see who the enemy is that you are fighting. We need to stop fighting ourselves and battle who the real enemy is!

We cannot live primarily by our feelings. We have to lead our feelings into compliance to God's Word. Our feelings can and will lie to us. Our emptiness can drive our feelings, so we must learn to live by what we know to be true, even if we feel we are not fully convinced yet.

Feelings are not evil; they just need to be trained in the way God designed them. As you grow in self-love, you will be able to see your feelings work for you not against you.

We are emotional beings that are capable of thinking and feeling. But the enemy can feed your thoughts, even sounding like your own voice. You can have negative thoughts coursing through your being without even realizing it. Ask God to raise your discernment so you can know when the garbage is talking.

As you grow in discernment, be aware of the accusing, condemning and guilt-ridden thoughts that come your way. They are designed to distract us from resting in God's love for us. The enemy is an accuser and will utilize a myriad of thoughts to keep us conflicted and blocked from self-love. Accusation, condemnation and guilt are not of God. They will never get us anywhere nor help us grow, but they will certainly demand for our attention.

Many believers get taken out by condemning thoughts, thinking God may be saying something in those reasonings. We must understand God's nature, for He does not use condemnation to get a point across to His children. Ever been on a guilt trip? God doesn't send believers on them; satan does.

As we remove condemnation from our frequency scanners, we gain the ability to receive from God. Condemnation is a "reception blocker" that prevents people from confidently receiving God's love. It will keep you in an unworthy state, where you remain blocked off from the fullness of God.

1 John 3:21 tells us that *if our heart does not condemn us, we have confidence toward God.* Masses of believers all over the world lack confidence when it comes to approaching God, because they live under the lie of condemnation. God responds to confident faith, but how can we approach Him confidently if we are so bogged down in feeling condemned, unworthy and not good enough?

Breaking condemnation allows us to stand confidently in obtaining what God has released to us. God is answering many prayers, but many are not receiving what they are asking for. Our loving Father is responding, but condemnation is blocking our ability to possess.

I encourage you to begin tearing down condemnation from your thoughts. Renounce it from your life and position yourself to receive. You are worthy because Jesus Christ makes us worthy to be called children of God. Do not let the enemy ruin your ability to be blessed by God for one more second.

3. Give yourself permission to walk free through a process. If you make this decision now, you won't beat yourself up when it seems you haven't arrived into victory quicker. The enemy will tell you that you should have been free decades ago, in order to discourage you. There is nothing worse than being beaten up over a seeming lack of progress, when we are seeking to get free.

We love to believe for the instantaneous freedom moments in people's lives, but we often diminish the power of day to day overcoming. When we welcome the process, we become more kind and patient to ourselves, giving love more room to operate in our lives. Engaging a process mindset builds a capacity for long term change to take root.

The danger of lacking self-love is that it leaves a trail of a lot programming. We've become hard-wired to obey its leadings, therefore mind renewal is critical. What we focus on and how we focus on it is the key to change. After being used to pollution in our thoughts, we have to be intentional about the purifying mindsets we will need to focus on.

We need to allow ourselves time to grow. We can't rush it. We have to make way for a journey, not an instant destination. Renewal takes time, especially in areas that involve how we do relationships. We have been so deeply trained to be ok with not loving ourselves and even allowing abusive thoughts to remain. It will take time to make those changes.

Can we be ok with the fact that we are in process? If so, we have just engaged the power of loving ourselves. I remind myself daily, "I am not who I was yesterday. I am daily changing step by step."

4. Grieve over your broken heart without living in pity. When it comes to self-love battles, so many have never grieved their pain or processed through difficult emotions. When those areas come to the surface, people want a quick Band-Aid so they can continue living in their dysfunctional patterns.

I am not promoting victimization, but I have found it to be very healthy for our hearts to acknowledge brokenness and grieve. There is something very special about someone who can come to grips with their pain and let it enhance their growth. It is possible to address what we did and did not experience that pierced us without having to go into pity.

So how do we grieve brokenness without it becoming pity ridden or driven by a victim mindset? *By not staying there.* Let the tears fall and let the grieving happen. Only God knows how long it will take. Some need a few days, others months. A great gift of love is giving yourself permission to live in process.

At some point in the grieving, you will need to make the exchange with God and let the healing flow. Don't allow yourself to remain any longer in this stage than you need to, but it's important not to rush it. It's amazing how having a "good cry" can be very beneficial to our being. An amazing exchange can be made with God when we weep tears of sadness, grief and pain before Him and give those feelings to Him.

I have found some of the greatest healing in the midst of great sadness, disappointment and tears. It is then, that a special peace and comfort manifests from the Holy Spirit. I receive a calm and confidence that everything is going to be ok. I also gain confidence in being more than a conqueror. I believe that those who know how to address pain in their lives will be able to access the blessing of joy, excitement and true happiness in dynamic ways.

Many live sheltered from pain and avoid it at all costs. Yet these same folks cannot engage true joy either. They need a high or some kind of circumstance to help their day-to-day mood. I often find that by allowing ourselves to address brokenness, we gain access to jewels on the other side.

Another way we can keep from becoming a victim in our pain is to make firm decisions. What action or step can we take to move from our pain into a healthier place? What can I learn from what I have been through? In what ways can I respond in a healed way? What new mindsets need to be cultivated? How can I help others who have been through what I have experienced?

5. Identify the mindsets you have struggled with that keep you from loving yourself. This exercise can be very helpful. Once we can identify the mindsets that we have been more vulnerable to, we can then detect them quicker when they rise up in our thoughts. Most ways of thinking that block us from love go undetected, so exposing them to the love and truth of God will give you greater leverage for victory.

I found it helpful to put names and labels to these battles. Just like when I took words out of the dictionary, I have found that putting a name to the enemy I am facing helps me to take more authority in my thoughts and become empowered to not just listen to every thought I have.

Take a moment to write down the key themes you struggle with. Here is a list of the most common thought patterns for your consideration.

Fear	Self-Condemnation
Self-Rejection	Self-Accusation
Self-Hatred	Anger
Unworthiness	Self-Pity

6. Begin breaking agreement with the mindsets that keep you from loving yourself. It is important that we firmly break agreement with mindsets that block us from loving ourselves. In order to break agreement, we need to utilize the power of repentance.

Repentance is a God-given tool to break the chains that bind us. We are held captive by that which has agreement in us. Repentance breaks the agreement. It gives us leverage to tell the enemy to get out of our life. When we repent of a destructive mindset, we break agreements we have with its ways.

Repentance in a very practical sense means: *to move from one way of thinking and into another*. We leave the enemy's thoughts and move into God's thinking. The first part of repentance means to change your spiritual way of thinking. It means that you have recognized something within you that is not of God and you want to address it. You have recognized it and you have taken responsibility for it. Now you are ready to change your thinking.

The enemy loses his hold when we repent, for in it we set a new direction for our lives. It is important that when exercising repentance, we do it out loud. As an example, a good start is saying, "God I repent for allowing self-hatred to be a part of my life."

As we move into the new direction, we begin to think in new ways that are loving to ourselves. This embeds the second part of repentance. I find that continually breaking agreement builds momentum over time, the more I practice it.

The following is a prayer that I have found to be helpful with many people that I have helped. It positions our hearts for breaking agreement and to stand in a place of declarative authority. My goal is to empower you to take love back and walk in the freeing power of Christ. I use the following ministry tool to help them focus their words for greatest breakthrough. Whatever word describes your battle, place it in the blanks and say it out loud.

PRAYER TO BREAK AGREEMENT

Father God, I thank You that love is available today. You are love, so I embrace You in Your love today.

Father, I recognize that I have had _____ in my life.

I take responsibility to be free from _____ in my generations.

I repent of and renounce the ways of _____.

Father, I receive your cleansing work to heal my heart in Your love.

I receive your love. I receive your forgiveness for not living in Your love. I forgive myself.

I ask today that _____ be broken and removed from my life in Jesus name.

Father, I ask that you fill the place where _____ has been and fill that place with your love, grace and goodness.

Today, I make a decision to love myself as God loves me.

I command all works of the enemy that seek to keep me from love to be removed from my life in Jesus name.

I command the mindsets of _____ to leave today.

Today, I declare myself free to love myself.

7. Forgive those who did not love you properly. There are two kinds of people that are important to forgive. The first are those that did not love you but should have. The second group involves those who wounded you by their direct actions towards you.

If you took a moment to look back, there were people who did not love you properly. It affected you to some degree, whether you acknowledge it or not. As we process through the pain, it is a fact that we have been wounded by those who should have loved us, but did not. We have also been affected by those who manifested unloving and abusive ways. Those things were wrong and not of God.

But we cannot love ourselves without forgiving others. We cannot expect to get healed and free while holding bitterness against those who wronged us. If we hold on to it, we drink our own poison. Love will remain a distant experience.

Forgiveness starts with dad and mom. They operated with the tools they were given in life. Some helped you while others didn't. This is the time to begin forgiving them so you can move on in your life and walk free.

I find the best way to do this is to out loud, forgive them specifically, in order to engage heart connection to the forgiveness. Don't just pray, "God I forgive dad and mom." Instead, pray prayers that are more focused, like, "I forgive you dad for abandoning me, for not telling me you loved me, for abusing my mom." Or, "I forgive you mom for not nurturing me, for giving me the silent treatment, for not standing up for me when dad was abusive."

Saying it like this cuts to the issues of the heart. When we forgive, we not only release them, we also release ourselves from the bondage.

Probably, one of the hardest people to forgive is ourselves. We beat ourselves up, as some kind of penance for our failures and mistakes. This dilutes the power of the cross, which gives us the ability to walk free from the torment of sin. God is not condemning us. The enemy is. God is a God of forgiveness, but we must receive it.

We cannot hold ourselves to the negative recall of the past anymore. Guilt and shame need to be cast down. When we do forgive ourselves, we come into alignment with God's love and acceptance of us.

8. Leave childhood ways and move into spiritual maturity. Many personal battles have ties to areas where we are still living as children and not moving into maturity. Our junk can be connected to childhood patterns that we have not broken away from.

In fact, I find that many adults have never officially "left father and mother" like the Bible says. I believe this is a crucial transition into adulthood whether you get married or not.

I remember a long time ago, I was in counseling for battles with anxiety and panic attacks. One of the things my therapist asked was, "Why do you still live with your parents?" I was more thinking of it from a financial standpoint. I was focusing on saving money. But he was referring to my emotional development of leaving my dad and mom to walk in the identity of who God says that I am. This was a great step in my spiritual development.

Many people leave home, but they don't leave their family's

dysfunctional ways. They often carry the baggage, keeping them from walking into the maturity that love invites them into.

Self-love struggles can also be sustained through our parents not releasing us. In fact, marriages can often struggle because the couple never left father and mother spiritually.

You must know that the enemy likes to use dysfunctional family connections to drag us back into our old bondage. Some people need a season of space from their family, often to work out their struggles without interference. This can be a healthy thing if done with a right heart.

It is important to leave father and mother in a healthy way to break the ties we have to self-love struggles. It may just be as simple as declaring it. It may mean establishing boundaries. Even if your relationship with family is amazing, this step still needs to be done. Don't do it with dishonor or bitterness. But once you grow up to adulthood, your relationship with Dad and Mom changes. It is now time to walk in a new season. This is especially critical if you want to stop your parent's voices from echoing in your head.

9. Break relational ties with toxic people who have bonded you with self-love struggles. We all have relationships that bind us to good or destructive patterns. Relational connections are meant to unify us with each other. God works in the power of unified relationship to release His power and love. At the same time, relational bonds can be formed to unify the enemy's work in our lives.

I often work with people who have left toxic people but are still carrying the bondage that developed in that relationship. This is because there is still a tie, keeping that person bound to the old patterns. I often find it helpful for the person to break the relational tie, through prayer and forgiveness. It is also helpful to step away from any habits that tie us to the old relationship or even objects that were shared together. This can be done effectively in the counsel of a mature person and through prayer.

It is often said that we are the average of all the main relationships we cultivate. The enemy would want to keep you around people that will not challenge you to grow, but hold you in patterns of bondage. Surrounding ourselves with people that want to be healthy will add fuel to your freedom journey.

There are probably some relationships you need to let go of today. There are people that you're trying to fix that need to be released and toxic people that are pulling you down into dysfunction. Out of love for ourselves, we have to respect who we are and begin moving on from relationships that are unhealthy and going nowhere.

I watch so many people stay in relationships with the hopes that someday the person will change or have a light bulb experience. They may end up waiting their whole life. We cannot expect God to heal us while we remain around people who are content to live in spiritual sludge.

From a place of self-love, we need to move away from people that reinforce our old self-junk and forge out to discover new relationships that are looking to grow and mature in love. You need people that are going to encourage the power of self-love in your life, brothers and sisters that will respect and empower you. Stop wasting your time on people that are selfish, self-consumed and unable to walk with you to higher levels.

We are the product of our relationships. They will either take us to new levels or hold us back. In the context of healthy relationships, our self-esteem and self-worth actually improves. Some people just need some new relationships to remind them of their God-given potential.

Sometimes we are afraid to step out into new relationships, because just being around successful people can make us feel bad about ourselves. This reveals the low level in which we see ourselves. We have to see that we are worth being around people that will sharpen us.

I have practiced this all my life, because certain friendships don't want to move into healthy directions. This is ok, because not every friend is going to go all the way with you. Some friends are for a season and some don't pace with you in your growth journey. I have also found that in certain seasons, I am a little more alone, because I made the choice to move on from some disempowering relationships and I am in the process of developing new ones. That transition takes time to complete. We just have to be patient.

10. Take action to value and accept yourself. It is time that in your posture and words, you begin to love and accept yourself more fully. Take a step forward and determine to make that a foundation in your life. If you don't love yourself, you won't be able to receive love from others and you will sabotage relationships.

You will need to take action in order to make this personal. Maybe it means standing in front of the mirror longer and complimenting yourself. It may be taking time to go get a new outfit or take time for more solitude. It may mean taking more time to rest or to pursue some form of personal development.

I encourage you to make a list of action steps you can take to love yourself. It will include words you say, decisions you make and habits you form. It may involve something as simple as giving yourself a hug every day. I often smile at myself in the mirror to kill any self-hate that will want to rise up. There are thousands of things you can do, but you will know as you talk to God, what action will mean the most for you.

_____

_____

_____

_____

_____

_____

For me, it was changing my nutritional habits to love myself, rather than being destructive and careless in my eating patterns. I changed when I went to bed and when I woke up. I spent more time looking in the mirror and liking what I saw. I took time to be still. I went for more walks. I took time to take care of myself and I encourage my wife to do the same. I laugh more and focus on not taking myself so seriously. We are no good to the world if we don't love ourselves in thought and action.

For those of you on social media, start by taking a great selfie picture of yourself and posting it to your account. Stop posting pictures of your kids, your dog and scenery as your profile picture. Put a great profile picture of you looking into the camera and giving a great smile. This is another very practical way to break through self-love barriers.

If you ask people to write down a list of their closest friends, they never think to write themselves. But next to God, we should live as our own first best friend. The enemy hates it when we come to peace and learn to love ourselves. One of the greatest ways we can learn to become our own best friend is to make our time alone fruitful. We spend 24 hours a day with ourselves, we might as well make it powerful.

Many people hate being alone, because they have not cultivated a healthy inner life regarding how they see themselves. Those who love themselves properly have no difficulty being alone or being in solitude. They use solitude as time to encourage and build themselves up.

11. Zero in on what God says about you every day. What we focus on grows and forms the story we associate with everything in our lives. Spiritual warriors learn to develop a laser-sharp focus in their thought life. With so many voices in the world, we have to narrow down what we choose to listen to. The battle for our hearts occurs between our ears, in what we listen to and allow to become the narrative for our lives.

Loving ourselves involves believing what God says about us, once and for all. We do this by determining what our focus will be. By repetitively focusing our thoughts on His love for us, we make way for love to have its fullest effect in our lives.

This will not come automatically, but only by intention. The goal is to make yourself one with God's thoughts. True belief is ours when who God is and what He says, manifests through our being.

Most people agree in theory with what God says, but it doesn't translate into their day-to-day thoughts and perceptions.

It takes continuous habits of focusing on what God says, for it to truly become a belief system.

To maintain this focus, I encourage people to find daily habits to remind themselves of what God says about them. We learn to believe what God says about us by finding great ways to remind ourselves of what His Word says. I encourage you to use everything you can to reinforce God's thoughts over you and remind yourself daily of them. We as humans leak easily. We think in one way and forget about it in minutes. We need to be reminded all the time.

That is why God told Israel to build memorials and to write on the doorposts. All these acts served as reminders to who God is and His involvement in the lives of His people. So don't wait to do this. Start now putting down reminders of what you need to remember.

It may be daily reminders on your phone. Journal entries can be very powerful. Some use note cards. Put them all over the house. At times, I have recorded a voice mail for myself so I would check it and be reminded. Keep it simple. Remind yourself about the thoughts that empower you and bring your focus to living in love fully.

12. Speak loving and empowering words to yourself every day. This practice has saved my life and the lives of many. Remember, when we are stuck in our junk, we often stop speaking out God's truth; therefore, the enemy gets to speak while we sit in silent defeat. That has to change for freedom to remain. Remember, silence can sometimes be affirmation to what the enemy is saying. We turn the tide by using our mouths for victory.

Some think that talking to yourself is crazy, but personally, I think it's crazy if you don't. I talk to myself every day and you should too. Use words to love and accept yourself, right where you are. Confront your negative self-talk by establishing new speaking habits. Use your declarations and add to them regularly. Develop a daily arsenal of divine weapons against all attacks in your mind. Instead of waiting for what the enemy is going to do, take ground for your victory today by using your words.

Sometimes using your mouth to make a firm stance establishes who you are more firmly within you. Sometimes exposing what the enemy is saying out loud will crush his power over you. The powers of darkness become disempowered when exposed to the light.

13. Step out and accept love from people. You will not be able to get free in hiding, so get out there and connect to others. Allow your relationships to be the laboratory for your transformation. Instead of seeing your relationships as a threat, view them as opportunities to grow in what love means.

For many, it is time to get back into fellowship and make the effort to connect. Get out of isolation and learn the value in fellowship. Many say, "Mark, I have tried that and got burned. I am sick of it." That posture only empowers the resistance.

Yes, relationships take work. They often stretch us farther than we think we can ever go. But it is worth the effort to get into sincere, vulnerable and encouraging fellowship.

Do it, even when everything in you seems to be screaming, "NO!" Face your fears, especially your relational fears. Move out of passivity and into faith so that you can receive from God through other people. Fear is never your friend. Behind every fear is an opportunity to be perfected in love.

I find that when it comes to self-love struggles, someone needs to love the resistance right out of you. Sometimes it takes a hug or an embrace that is pure. It may take someone looking you in the eyes and speaking love over you.

I remember the very day I was set free to feel safe in relationships. I got free from self-hate that day and it wasn't at an altar or a church service. It was at a friend's house, where we were having dinner. There wasn't anything out of the ordinary happening, nor did the hosts do anything special in particular. It was simply a night to enjoy some barbeque and nice weather. But that night I felt a new level of freedom breakthrough in me while sitting at dinner. I looked over at my wife and whispered, "Hey...guess what. Something broke off of me. I'm free...."

It was because of the investment I made to live in freedom. It was at that moment that it broke, and I knew it. That garbage finally left and I was free. But it was because of the daily investment that this moment paid off. Relationships are hard work, but they are the environments where we practice our freedom walk.

14. Submit to healthy discipline. True discipline is a part of the language of love. It involves two practices.

First, we need to submit ourselves to healthy leaders that can speak into our lives and help us make adjustments where needed. Because so many of us have been damaged by spiritual leaders in the past, we tend to avoid them all together. But we cannot avoid the blind spots in life by ourselves. God works through leadership structure to bless our lives, even though they may be flawed and broken.

I am not saying tolerate abuse. There are healthy leaders and coaches out there; you just need to find them. Don't rush it. Be intentional about finding people who can have your back spiritually and speak into your life. I am not just talking about people who correct you, but healthy leaders who are equipped to empower you into the next level of your journey.

God cannot deal with us as sons and daughters if we do not know how to handle correction. Many people who struggle with a lack of self-love avoid intimacy with God altogether, because they fear the exposure of coming into His light. Yet they fail to know that His light is so loving and freeing.

God says in Hebrews 12 that if we cannot be disciplined and corrected, then we are living as illegitimate children. One of the signs of living in true sonship is our ability to receive correction from God and others. We grow and mature from it, but it takes a submissive heart to get there.

Second, we need to experience the power of a disciplined life. Self-love empowers us to live in discipline, where our days have more order and intention attached to them. When we lack self-love, we tend to just let our days coast by without having purpose. I know for me, I needed a daily regimen to keep me on track for my deliverance. I was no longer allowed to sleep till whenever I felt like getting up, for it encouraged me to stay in self-pity. I went to gatherings or outings even when I was struggling. I stopped avoiding people or situations that made me want to back away in my junk.

Discipline says, "I am going to do this because I love myself, whether I feel it or not." With discipline, we are committed to the long-term results and are swayed very little by the resistance that rises up.

When I first fought against self-love struggles, I had very up and down emotional days, which were intensified by my erratic schedule and undisciplined life. As I began to love myself more, I saw that regular eating schedules, daily routines and even my bedtime rituals were all ways I could love myself and care for who God made me to be.

15. Put away self-pity and victim living. If you have self-love struggles, then the enemy knows how to use self-pity to make you check out. Pity is the hook that drives us back and keeps us back in destructive patterns. I have watched many people get taken out from tremendous breakthrough chances because the enemy convinced them to check out at key opportune times.

I have had people I work with at the last minute get taken out emotionally, right when there was an event or conference coming, that would deal with the very issue they struggled with. Over and over again I have seen the enemy take people out right before that key breakthrough opportunity. He often uses self-pity to take them out emotionally and cause them to be so inward they can't see victory right in front of them.

To break self-pity, we have to ask ourselves, *do I really want to be free? Do I really want to be healed? Am I willing to do whatever it takes?* Because life will challenge us on this. Situations will come to take us out; giving us a reason to quit or to say *this is just all too hard.* It is in these moments that our answer to those questions really comes into play. Because honestly, some people enjoy their insanity and dysfunction. It's toxic, but they don't know any other way to live. Breaking self-pity invites courage to move into new life that welcomes breakthrough, healing, freedom and life transformation.

16. Reach out and love someone. Whenever we get stuck in our own garbage, the best thing to do is reach out and love on someone, rather than fall into self-loathing. Self-love does not mean we ignore others. In fact, whatever love we receive needs to flow out to other people we interact with.

What I am speaking about here is breaking those emotional spirals we can fall into, where we isolate and simmer in our bondage stew. The answer to feeling sorry for yourself is to go out and love on people–feed the sheep that Christ has called you to feed.

I find that if I get too focused on my problems, by helping someone else, it gets me out of selfishness and puts my issues in the right perspective. I am not ignoring my struggles. I am just not letting them own me. Sometimes seeing someone else's problems helps keep us from feeling sorry for ourselves.

A classic lie of the enemy is that you can't love someone unless you have perfectly arrived yourself. When I was in pastoring, there would be those who wouldn't get involved in service or helping others because they believed they weren't ready. They thought because they didn't love themselves perfectly, they were disqualified from helping others. This is a clear lie that took them out of great opportunities to grow.

17. Find actions that cultivate a healthy mood and state of mind. I really believe in the power of doing something physically to signal our inner man that change is in place. We often need to interrupt our dysfunctional patterns, to jar ourselves out of the funks we slide into. Certain actions can trigger us out of bondage and into more self-loving thinking. We may need to jolt ourselves out of introspection or from just being too much in our own head.

Sometimes it's as simple as "get moving." Many times some good exercise can help get positive neurotransmitters and endorphins firing. Those chemical signals will help us remain in healthy self-love. I often find a good walk can help shift my state of mind very quickly.

I have learned over the years that managing my daily mood is the most important thing I can watch over. My emotional state will determine how I will initially respond to everything that comes my way. Most people are not taken out by the hard circumstances they face, but the poor state of mind they have already.

I believe we need to watch over our mood continually. Being without self-love is the number one reason people struggle with their day to day mood. With this in mind, I schedule daily habits that reinforce a powerful mood and keep me growing in the fruit of the Spirit. How much sleep I get, my self-talk, what I eat, what I read, the kind of music I listen to, the friends I spend time with and the exercise I do, all contribute to place me in the best mood possible.

We often need to do things to snap us out of our funks. Sometimes I will kick on some music and start dancing in my house. I was never the dancing type, until I learned that dance was made for our freedom.

I like to laugh...a lot. Be sure to laugh every day, as much as possible. Studies show that the average child laughs anywhere from 300 to 500 times a day. Meanwhile, the average adult laughs only about 15 times a day.[1] Growing up, we all started taking ourselves way too seriously. No wonder we are filled with toxic thinking!

I recommend you work to restore laughter in your life. Maybe you need to weep and grieve, but laughter is coming soon, sooner than you think. Don't wait until everything is perfect to laugh. Start now, because the joy of the Lord is your strength!

Take risks. Try something new. Make a new relationship. Develop a new skill. Get out there and shake this self-garbage off your life. Do a new activity that will stretch you and snap you out of self-protection. Get out there and dance!

Key: When you see yourself, God wants you to like what you see! Be ready to take your life back! Get out there and be loved!

Love has been perfected among us in this: that we may have boldness in the day of judgment; because as He is, so are we in this world. There is no fear in love; but perfect love casts out fear, because fear involves torment. But he who fears has not been made perfect in love. We love Him because He first loved us. 1 John 4:17-19

GO LOVE AND BE LOVED.

---

[1] http://www.medicalcenter.virginia.edu/feap/work-life/newsletters/Humor%20and%20Stress.pdf

You say: It's impossible
God says: All things are possible
You say: I'm too tired
God says: I will give you rest
You say: Nobody really loves me.
God says: I love you
You say: I can't go on
God says: My grace is sufficient
You say: I cannot figure things out
God says: I will direct your steps
You say: I can't do it
God says: You can do all things through Christ
You say: I can't forgive myself
God says: Receive my forgiveness and you'll be able forgive others
You say: I can't manage
God says: I can supply all your needs
You say: I am afraid
God says: I have not given you fear and I love you
You say: I am always worried and frustrated
God says: Cast ALL your cares on me
You say: I am not smart enough
God says: I give you wisdom
You say: I feel all alone
God says: I will never leave you or forsake you
- Author Unknown

A RELATIONSHIP WITH GOD

1. **God loves you very dearly and has an amazing purpose and plan for your life.**

   We love Him because He first loved us. 1 John 4:19

   For God so loved the world that He gave His only begotten Son, that whoever believes in Him should not perish but have everlasting life. John 3:16

   The thief does not come except to steal, and to kill, and to destroy. I have come that they may have life, and that they may have it more abundantly. John 10:10

2. **Because of sin, man is separated from God and cannot know and experience His love and purposes.**

   for all have sinned and fall short of the glory of God. Romans 3:23

   For the wages of sin is death, but the gift of God is eternal life in Christ Jesus our Lord. Romans 6:23

3. **Jesus Christ came to earth and died on the cross for our sins. He rose from the dead and is the only way to a relationship with God. Through Jesus, we can know God's love and purpose for our life.**

   But God demonstrates His own love toward us, in that while we were still sinners, Christ died for us. Romans 5:8

   Jesus said to him, "I am the way, the truth, and the life. No one comes to the Father except through Me. John 14:6

4. **Jesus invites us to open up to God and have an intimate relationship with Him.**

   Behold, I stand at the door and knock. If anyone hears My voice and opens the door, I will come in to him and dine with him, and he with Me. Revelation 3:20

5. **Our responsibility is to believe and receive Jesus Christ as our Savior and Lord.**

   But as many as received Him, to them He gave the right to become children of God, to those who believe in His name. John 1:12

6. **When we receive Christ, we do so by faith, believing in what He did on the cross, not on our own ability or works.**

   For by grace you have been saved through faith, and that not of yourselves; it is the gift of God, not of works, lest anyone should boast. Ephesians 2:8-9

7. **You can receive Christ now by faith and enter into a new relationship with God through prayer.**

   If you confess with your mouth the Lord Jesus and believe in your heart that God has raised Him from the dead, you will be saved. For with the heart one believes unto righteousness, and with the mouth confession is made unto salvation. For the Scripture says, "Whoever believes on Him will not be put to shame." For there is no distinction between Jew and Greek, for the same Lord over all is rich to all who call upon Him. For "whoever calls on the name of the Lord shall be saved." Romans 10:9-13

Here is a suggested prayer:

Father I come to You in the name of Jesus Christ and I thank You for sending Your Son to die for me. Jesus, I recognize my need for You. I thank You for dying on the cross for my sins, and I open my heart to You right now. I receive your forgiveness for my sins and I thank You for giving me eternal life. I receive You as my Savior and Lord. I invite You to come in and be Lord of my life. Show me Your love and lead me to become the person You want me to be. I receive the Father's love and my adoption as Father God's child.

If this prayer echoes the desire of your heart, I invite you to pray it right now and Jesus will come into your life, as He promised.

SCRIPTURES

Psalm 139:14-16 (NIV) *I praise you because I am fearfully and wonderfully made; your works are wonderful; I know that full well. My frame was not hidden from you when I was made in the secret place, when I was woven together in the depths of the earth. Your eyes saw my unformed body; all the days ordained for me were written in your book before one of them came to be.*

Ephesians 2:10 *For we are His workmanship, created in Christ Jesus for good works, which God prepared beforehand that we should walk in them.*

Genesis 1:26-27 *Then God said, "Let Us make man in Our image, according to Our likeness; let them have dominion over the fish of the sea, over the birds of the air, and over the cattle, over all the earth and over every creeping thing that creeps on the earth." So God created man in His [own] image; in the image of God He created him; male and female He created them.*

Romans 8:29-31 *For whom He foreknew, He also predestined [to be] conformed to the image of His Son, that He might be the firstborn among many brethren. Moreover, whom He predestined, these He also called; whom He called, these He also justified; and whom He justified, these He also glorified. What then shall we say to these things? If God [is] for us, who [can be] against us?*

Jeremiah 1:5 *Before I formed you in the womb I knew you; Before you were born I sanctified you; I ordained you a prophet to the nations.*

Isaiah 43:4 *Since you were precious in My sight, You have been honored, And I have loved you; Therefore I will give men for you, And people for your life.*

Isaiah 49:15-16 *Can a woman forget her nursing child, And not have compassion on the son of her womb? Surely they may forget,*

Yet I will not forget you. See, I have inscribed you on the palms [of My hands]; Your walls [are] continually before Me.

Isaiah 62:3-5 *You shall also be a crown of glory In the hand of the LORD, and a royal diadem In the hand of your God. You shall no longer be termed Forsaken, nor shall your land any more be termed desolate; But you shall be called Hephzibah, and your land Beulah; For the LORD delights in you, and your land shall be married. For [as] a young man marries a virgin, [So] shall your sons marry you; And [as] the bridegroom rejoices over the bride, [So] shall your God rejoice over you.*

Psalms 35:27 *Let them shout for joy and be glad, Who favor my righteous cause; And let them say continually, "Let the LORD be magnified, who has pleasure in the prosperity of His servant."*

Zephaniah 3:17 *The LORD your God in your midst, The Mighty One, will save; He will rejoice over you with gladness, He will quiet [you] with His love, He will rejoice over you with singing.*

Ephesians 5:28-30 *So husbands ought to love their own wives as their own bodies; he who loves his wife loves himself. For no one ever hated his own flesh, but nourishes and cherishes it, just as the Lord [does] the church. For we are members of His body, of His flesh and of His bones.*

Psalm 16:3 *As for the saints who [are] on the earth, "They are the excellent ones, in whom is all my delight."*

2 Corinthians 6:16 *For you are the temple of the living God. As God has said: "I will dwell in them, and walk among them. I will be their God, And they shall be My people."*

1 Corinthians 3:16,17 *Do you not know that you are the temple of God and [that] the Spirit of God dwells in you? If anyone defiles the temple of God, God will destroy him. For the temple of God is holy, which [temple] you are.*

1 Corinthians 6:19-20 *Or do you not know that your body is the* temple of the Holy Spirit [who is] in you, whom you have from God, and you are not your own? For you were bought at a price; therefore glorify God in your body and in your spirit, which are God's.

2 Peter 1:4 *As His divine power has given to us all things that [pertain] to life and godliness, through the knowledge of Him who called us by glory and virtue, by which have been given to us exceedingly great and precious promises, that through these you may be partakers of the divine nature, having escaped the corruption [that is] in the world through lust.*

2 Corinthians 5:21 *For He made Him who knew no sin [to be] sin for us, that we might become the righteousness of God in Him.*

Malachi 3:17 *"They shall be Mine," says the LORD of hosts, "on the day that I make them My jewels. And I will spare them as a man spares his own son who serves him."*

OTHER BOOKS BY MARK DEJESUS

For more information regarding Turning Hearts Ministries:
TurningHeartsMinistries.org
For more information on Mark DeJesus & Transformed You:
MarkDeJesus.com

Made in the USA
Columbia, SC
07 September 2023

22593986R00117